175
High-Impact
Cover Letters

175
HIGH-IMPACT
COVER LETTERS

THIRD EDITION

Richard H. Beatty

John Wiley & Sons, Inc.

This book is printed on acid-free paper. ∞

Copyright © 2002 by Richard H. Beatty. All rights reserved.

Published by John Wiley & Sons, Inc., New York.
Published simultaneously in Canada.

This publication is designed to provide accurate and authoritative information in regard to the subject matter covered. It is sold with the understanding that the publisher is not engaged in rendering professional services. If professional advice or other expert assistance is required, the services of a competent professional person should be sought.

Library of Congress Cataloging-in-Publication Data:

Beatty, Richard H., 1939–
    175 high-impact cover letters / Richard H. Beatty.— 3rd ed.
      p. cm.
    Includes index.
    ISBN 0-471-21084-6 (pbk. : alk. paper)
    1. Cover letters. 2. Job hunting. I. Title: One hundred seventy-five high-impact cover letters. II. Title.

    HF5383 .B324 2002
    650.14′2—dc21

                           2001046963

Printed in the United States of America.

10 9 8 7 6 5 4 3 2

To the legions of job seekers who, during my years as an
employment executive, sent me thousands-upon-thousands
of cover letters and resumes.

I have seen them all, both the good and the bad! You helped me
appreciate what a truly good cover letter can do for the job seeker.

Thank you!

Preface

One of the truly arduous tasks of running a successful job-hunting campaign is consistently writing effective cover letters. For most people, this proves a difficult and ever-present challenge. Unlike a resume, where the job seeker can commit several hours to its perfection, cover letters must often be written "on the run," be tailored to specific circumstances, and still have a highly positive impact on the reader. For most people, this presents a difficult challenge. Unfortunately, in many cases, a hurried, sloppily-prepared cover letter can lead to disastrous results!

The cover letter is far too important to be left to chance or hurriedly written at the last minute. Instead, the job seeker needs to be equipped ahead of time with an arsenal of highly effective, professional cover letter models that, with only minor modification, can be rapidly deployed as needed.

This book provides the job seeker with just such an arsenal! It contains 175 highly effective cover-letter samples that, with slight modification, can be rapidly deployed by the job seeker throughout the job-hunting campaign. These letters have been designed to meet a wide range of circumstances commonly faced by the job seeker, equipping him or her with the ability to quickly respond with a well-written, professional document that creates a favorable impression and enhances one's employment candidacy.

Throughout the book, the reader is furnished with specific instructions for preparation of each type of cover letter, followed by numerous letter examples to assist in their preparation. Five different cover letter types are presented, including: (1) the employer broadcast letter, (2) the search firm broadcast letter, (3) the advertising response letter, (4) the networking cover letter, and (5) the resume letter. A full chapter, along with 30 or more model letters, has been dedicated to each of the five letter types.

Chapter 4, on advertising response letters, should prove particularly helpful to the job seeker. This chapter contains some 30 sample cover letters positioned opposite the advertisements to which they were designed to respond. By comparing each sample advertisement and its corresponding cover letter, readers quickly see how to construct an efficient, high-impact cover letter specifically tailored to the employer's needs.

Also provided is a chapter on the resume letter, a cross between the cover letter and the resume document. The resume letter is sometimes used as a substitute for the resume itself. A well-designed resume letter is easy to read, provides a brief but excellent synopsis of the writer's credentials, and sometimes stimulates sufficient interest to warrant a job interview, without forcing the employer to read a lengthy resume.

Chapter 7 covers the subject of thank-you letters, an important topic too often ignored by most books on employment letters. Although not truly a cover letter, a well-crafted thank-you letter deserves a special place of honor in the cover-letter arsenal. If well designed and sent immediately upon return from the job interview, this letter can have a highly positive impact on the employer's hiring decision. Besides simply affirming the author's good manners, it also provides an excellent marketing opportunity to further reinforce one's value to prospective employers.

A new chapter, Chapter 8, now provides the reader with some "do's" and "don'ts" when it comes to effective cover letter writing. This serves as an excellent last-minute checklist before finalizing the cover letter and mailing it.

In this Third Edition, I have also rewritten and fine-tuned most of the cover letter samples, bringing them up-to-date with the most current thinking and the terminology now used in the staffing field. And, finally, a recent, authoritative survey of nearly 600 employment professionals, conducted by the Society for Human Resource Management, provides some excellent data supporting many of the cover letter opinions and recommendations of this author. This survey is appropriately referenced in the text and affirms much of what I believe is important to effective cover letter construction.

With its step-by-step instructions and 175 high-impact cover-letter samples, this book should greatly simplify the challenge of cover-letter writing for most job seekers. It gives readers all the ammunition necessary to write highly effective, professional letters that are sure to enhance the effectiveness and impact of their job-hunting campaign.

Best wishes for a successful job search and rewarding career.

RICHARD H. BEATTY

West Chester, Pennsylvania
January 2002

Contents

1

Importance of Cover Letters

The cover letter you choose for transmitting your resume to an employer or important networking contact can be one of the most significant factors in the success (or failure) of your job-hunting campaign. In fact, a survey of nearly 600 employment professionals, conducted by the Society for Human Resource Management (SHRM), suggests some 76% of employers may automatically eliminate an employment candidate from any further hiring consideration, based solely on the quality of his or her cover letter alone. Further, 43% of survey respondents also reported they view the cover letter as equal to the resume in importance. When it comes to running an effective employment campaign, therefore, this data should cause you to sit up and take notice! (*Note:* A copy of the full survey, which covers both cover letters and resumes can be obtained by contacting SHRM by phone, (703) 548-3440, or by e-mail at SHRM.org.)

If well written and informative, the cover letter can grab the reader's attention, raise his curiosity, and stimulate immediate interest in your employment candidacy. In fact, if particularly well written, it can sometimes raise sufficient interest to compel the reader to extend an interview invitation without reading the resume document to which it is attached.

By contrast, a poorly written cover letter can be disastrous to an otherwise successful job-hunting campaign, serving as an immediate roadblock to any further consideration of your employment candidacy. The way it is organized, what it says, how it is stated, what is included/excluded, what is highlighted/emphasized—all are critical factors impacting cover-letter effectiveness. Cover letters that are poorly conceived and fail to give due consideration to these important factors can (and will) prove devastating, causing employers to discard both the cover letter and the companion resume accompanying it.

As an employment professional, with years of experience, I am continuously amazed that people will invest hours (or sometimes days) in the preparation and design of the "perfect" resume, yet spend little or no time writing the cover letter that serves as the overlay document that introduces their employment resume and summary of professional credentials. This is the print equivalent of wearing a dirty, rumpled, ill-fitting suit over a well-starched, clean, white shirt to the job interview.

Let's face it, the cover letter is the very first thing that greets the reader's eye. And there has been a great deal written about the importance of "first impressions" during the employment and interview process. The cover letter is no exception! It is the document that creates that all-important first impression, and can have a great deal of impact on how the reader "perceives" you right from the start.

If the cover letter is neat and well-written, it creates a positive impression, suggesting you are equally conscientious and fastidious about your work. Conversely, if sloppy or poorly written, the cover letter suggests you are someone who has little professional pride.

Besides appearance, what you say in the cover letter (and how you say it) can have considerable impact on the reader. Such factors immediately tell the reader something about your general communication skills. For example, they telegraph whether you are expressive, concise, articulate, and generally an effective communicator—or whether you are inexpressive, overly detailed, inarticulate, or generally have poor communication skills. These factors (that is, what you say and how you say it) can also telegraph something about your intellectual capacity and ability to think. For example, they can suggest to the reader that you are conceptual, strategic, analytical, logical, or (if the letter is not carefully choreographed) that your thinking is muddled, overly simplistic, illogical, and disorganized.

Finally, if well designed, the cover letter will "pre-market" your candidacy. If, as a result of reading your cover letter, for example, the reader is feeling positive and impressed, these feelings will typically spill over into the resume, which will then be read with a less critical eye. Conversely, if the cover letter is poorly written, your resume is likely not to be read at all.

Although perhaps difficult to believe, I have had prominent people tell me they place more stock in the cover letter than they do the resume. Some have said they invited candidates for employment interviews based solely on the strength of their cover letter alone, without regard to the resume. Although I find his equally amazing, some even volunteered they seldom bother to read the resume if the cover letter is impressive.

Considering such overwhelming evidence, we can only conclude that the cover letter is a very important document indeed. How it is designed and written can make a significant difference in job-hunting success. Your cover letters deserve deliberate and careful attention if you wish to maximize your opportunities in the marketplace. This book, if carefully followed, should provide you with a distinct competitive advantage, when it comes to producing high-impact cover letters that will stimulate interest in your employment candidacy.

TYPES OF COVER LETTERS

When most people think about cover letters, they have in mind the letter that is used to transmit their resume to a prospective employer. Actually, there are five types of cover letters, each designed a little differently and each having a slightly different purpose. These are:

1. Letters to Employers.
2. Letters to Search Firms.
3. Advertising Response Letters.
4. Networking Cover Letters.
5. Resume Letters.

This book will thoroughly familiarize you with each of these letter types and provide you with numerous examples as the basis for modeling and writing your own cover letter. By carefully studying these sample letters and following the instructions provided at the beginning of each chapter, you will have all you need to write a highly effective cover letter and add a good deal of zest and positive impact to your job-hunting campaign.

2

Letters to Employers

If you are contemplating use of a mass-mailing program to send your resume to employers, you will be playing a bit of a "numbers game." Although a staple of most well-planned job-hunting campaigns, such mass mailings seldom produce significant results when compared to other, more productive job-hunting sources, such as networking, recruitment advertising, and employment agencies. Nonetheless, should you elect to use the direct-mail approach, you will need an effective cover letter to help you realize a reasonable return on the time and money you invest in this process.

Professionals who specialize in the direct-mail business expect a well-executed, direct-mail campaign will normally generate a return in the 3% to 5% range. Thus, a targeted mailing of 300 letters should generate about 9 to 15 responses. If you are planning to utilize this approach as part of your job search program, your mailing should target several hundred firms.

In a tight labor market, characterized by high unemployment and a glut of available candidates on the market, the direct-mail approach can be even less effective. Research conducted during such a market, for example, has shown a positive response rate of only about 3%. Further, some knowledgeable employment experts feel that the rate of return is likely to be even lower, depending on the severity of market conditions.

When considering whether to utilize direct mail as part of your job-hunting program, the important thing to remember is that it takes only a *single* favorable response to generate a job interview. If it's the right job, this approach can pay off handsomely, providing you with the career opportunity of a lifetime!

Don't be discouraged by the meager statistical results cited here. Instead, be sure to make the direct-mail campaign a component of your overall job-search strategy. Just remember to maintain realistic expectations.

THE BROADCAST LETTER

In the parlance of employment professionals, the cover letter used by job seekers to transmit their resumes to prospective employers is commonly known as a *broadcast* letter. This name comes from use of the letter to *broadcast* the candidate's employment availability to a large audience of employers.

The composition of the broadcast letter is extremely important to the outcome of your direct-mail campaign. If well designed and written, it will improve your response rate and substantially increase the number of interview opportunities presented to you. Conversely, if poorly written, it will detract from mailing results and greatly reduce (or even eliminate) your opportunities for employment interviews.

So, if you are going to assure yourself of an effective direct-mail campaign, you will want to spend some quality time in designing a well-written cover letter that will successfully market your skills and capabilities to prospective employers.

LIST OF TARGET COMPANIES AND MANAGERS

Wherever possible, your broadcast cover letter should be directed to a specific individual at each of your target firms. Research demonstrates such "personally targeted" mailings are looked upon more favorably by recipients and are more likely to produce a favorable response. This statement is backed by the SHRM cover letter survey, which reports that 69% of the employment professionals surveyed view such personalized cover letters more positively. A letter simply addressed to the "Manager of Manufacturing," without the manager's name, does not engender the same warm feelings on the part of the recipient and "just doesn't cut it" if you expect to maximize the results of your mailing campaign!

When you research your list of target companies, therefore, it is important to find the name and exact title of the individual you wish to target. When deciding who to target for mailing purposes, the rule-of-thumb is: Address the manager who is immediately above the person for whom you are likely to work. When it is not possible for you to identify this individual, target the top executive in charge of the overall function you have earmarked for job-search purposes.

National offices of industry and professional associations are often an excellent source for identifying reference books and automated lists of key personnel. A quick call to the association president can frequently identify the best research sources for producing the names and titles you need. You might also try a brief search on the Internet, which can sometimes produce the names of outstanding references for this kind of information.

A CARDINAL RULE

When preparing your direct-mail program, one cardinal rule to follow is, "Never mail your cover letter and resume to the human resources (or employment) department!" At first blush, this may sound like strange advice. However, these departments are often inundated with thousands of unsolicited resumes and are often simply not staffed to efficiently handle the huge volume of correspondence they receive.

Additionally, the human resources function is frequently only aware of the organization's "formal" job openings. That is, they may only know of those employment opportunities that have been formally approved by management. They may be totally unaware of "informal" or "hidden" employment openings—those that are in the minds of their client managers and have not yet been formally communicated.

This phenomenon of informal job opportunities has been called the "hidden job market." Estimates by career experts suggest the size of this hidden job market may well be 70% to 80% of the entire job market. Targeting your direct mail campaign to the human resources department could thus exclude you from employment consideration by a large percentage of the market.

Targeting your mailing directly to functional managers, rather than the human resources or employment function, by contrast, allows you to directly access the hidden job market. Receipt of your broadcast cover letter and accompanying resume by the functional manager can be just what it takes to stimulate interest in your candidacy and generate a job interview rather than the standard "no interest" letter typically sent by the human resources function.

This is why it is so important to target your letters to specific functional managers if you wish to maximize the results of your direct mail program and take full advantage of the benefits of the hidden job market.

THE VALUE-ADDED PROPOSITION

When designing your general broadcast cover letter, bear in mind that employers don't fill positions just for the sake of filling them. They are looking for productive candidates capable of accomplishing specific results—persons who can add true "value" to their organizations.

Careful analysis of the job content of your targeted position can often yield good clues as to the qualifications and contributions employers expect of a successful candidate. Good cover letter design highlights these qualifications as well as emphasizes the "value" you can bring to their organizations in these important areas. Answering the following questions should prove helpful in defining these areas:

1. What are the key, ongoing functional accountabilities of the position for which you are applying?
2. In each of these key functional areas, what are the end results desired by most employers?
3. What significant results have you achieved in each of these key results areas that will convince employers of the value you can bring to their function?

If just entering the job market for the first time, you will need a slightly different approach. You will want to focus on specific skills and attributes you possess that should enable you to perform the job particularly well. The following questions may help you to organize your thoughts on this matter:

1. What are the key problems you will need to solve if you are to be successful in performing your targeted job?

2. What key knowledge and/or skills will be required in order for you to solve these problems and achieve successful job performance?
3. Which of these qualifications (knowledge/skills) do you possess?
4. What evidence can you give of your ability to apply these qualities?
5. What personal attributes are considered important in successfully performing your targeted job?
6. Which of these attributes do you possess?
7. What evidence can you cite regarding these attributes?

The sample cover letters contained in this chapter will effectively illustrate how these key accomplishments or important personal traits can be highlighted to your advantage.

KEY ELEMENTS OF BROADCAST LETTER

Review of the sample cover letters provided in this chapter will reveal there are five key elements to effective broadcast cover letter composition:

1. An introductory paragraph that includes a statement of your job search objective.
2. A brief summary paragraph that summarizes your overall background and experience.
3. A "selling" (value-adding) paragraph that highlights specific results achieved by you in those areas known to be important to successful job performance.
4. A request for action on your candidacy.
5. A statement of appreciation for the employer's consideration of your employment candidacy.

Notice these key elements in the following cover letter samples that have been provided as models for designing your own effective direct-mail cover-letter campaign.

832 Harrington Way
Columbia, MD 16274

January 28, 2003

Mr. David R. Bradford
Director of Marketing
Marshall Foods, Inc.
100 Marshall Place
Racine, WI 54751

Dear Mr. Bradford:

I am writing to present my credentials for the position of Brand Manager, a position for which I am well qualified. I am confident that you will quickly recognize my ability to make major contributions to your company's marketing efforts.

As my resume will attest, I have earned an excellent reputation for pumping new life into old brands and accelerating their performance. Examples of my accomplishments in this area include:

- Tripled frozen pizza market share in only nine months

- Increased microwave popcorn market share by 75% in two years

- Improved direct mail orders of premium crackers by 42% in eighteen months through creative coupon approach

My contributions to new brands have been equally noteworthy. For example:

- Achieved 32% market share penetration for line of low salt shredded cheeses within one year of market introduction

- Completed national roll-out of "Snack Packs," a line of single-serving, fruit-flavored yogurt cups, in six months, reaching 22% market penetration

I am fully capable of making similar contributions to Marshall Foods in the marketing of either new products or existing brands.

Should you have room in your organization for a top-notch marketing professional capable of making immediate contributions to your marketing efforts and adding significant profit to your bottom line, please give me a call. I look forward to hearing from you.

Thank you for your consideration.

Sincerely,

Michelle J. Crompton

Michelle J. Crompton

MJC/rac

Enclosure

134 Dixon Hall, East
Dickinson University
Carlisle, PA 50311

January 15, 2004

Ms. Martha A. Bridgton
Director of Marketing and Sales
Harmon Industries, Inc.
85 Commerce Drive
Dayton, OH 66306

Dear Ms. Bridgton:

I am very interested in talking with you about employment as a Sales Representative Trainee with Harmon Industries, and hope you will give my candidacy strong consideration. I feel I have the necessary skills and interest to be an excellent contributor to your organization and would appreciate the opportunity to demonstrate this through a personal interview with your recruiter during Harmon's forthcoming recruiting schedule at Dickinson University. My resume is enclosed for your reference.

Although short on experience, Ms. Bridgton, I am long on effort and enthusiasm. I am an outgoing, friendly individual with the ability to build solid, lasting relationships with valued customers. My strong service orientation and bias for action would serve your company well in responding to the needs of your clients. My drive, determination and leadership abilities are well-evidenced by the following accomplishments:

- Grade Point Average of 3.6/4.0

- Fraternity President, Senior Year
- Fraternity Vice President, Junior Year
- Pledge Chairman, Sophomore Year

- Captain, Varsity Crew Team, Senior Year
- Member, Varsity Crew Team, 3 Years
- Co-Captain, Varsity Swim Team, Junior Year
- Member, Varsity Swim Team, 4 Years

I would like the chance to put my energy, drive and enthusiasm to work for a company such as yours. May I have the opportunity to further discuss your requirements during a personal meeting with your campus representative on February 18th?

Sincerely,

Bradford D. Lance

Bradford D. Lance

BDL/ael

Enclosure

ELAINE D. FISHER
35 Darwin Place
Fort Wayne, IN 55437

June 14, 2003

Mr. Karl F. Klauser
President and COO
Barton Metals, Inc.
200 Rockford Industrial Park
Indianapolis IN 60062

Dear Mr. Klauser:

As the Chief Operating Officer of a leading company in the metals refining industry, I know you are keenly aware of the value a top-notch manufacturing executive can deliver to a profit-oriented company such as yours. Should you be seeking a proven contributor to lead your refinery operations, therefore, I encourage you to seriously consider my credentials.

An operating executive holding an M.S. degree in Engineering and having over 15 years solid achievement and career progression, I have established an outstanding reputation as a strong profit contributor. Among some of my more notable accomplishments are:

- a 36% reduction in manufacturing costs in a major furnace operation (annual savings of $13 million)

- on-time and below cost start-up of a $435 million tube manufacturing plant (project savings of $7 million)

- a 28% reduction in labor costs over a three-plant operation through an extensive work redesign project (annual savings of $5.9 million)

- a 68% reduction in scrap and 86% reduction in customer complaints through implementation of an SPC-based total quality effort (annual savings of $4.8 million)

Perhaps we could meet to discuss the contributions I am capable of making as a senior member of your manufacturing team. Should you agree, I can be reached during office hours at (612) 737-2310 or at (612) 555-6731 in the evening.

Sincerely,

Elaine D. Fisher

Elaine D. Fisher

EDF/rms

Enclosure

120 Franklin Drive
Broomall, PA 19008

October 29, 2004

Dr. Stacey E. Evans
Vice President Research & Development
Elco Plastics, Inc.
425 Polymer Drive
Greenville, SC 30345

Dear Dr. Evans:

As one of the leaders in the field of polymer chemistry, Elco Plastics might be interested in a seasoned Product Development Chemist with a demonstrated record of achievement as a new product innovator in the world of plastics. My credentials include an M.S. in Polymer Chemistry with over 15 years research experience in the polymer industry.

As you can see from the enclosed resume, my reputation as a creative, innovator is well supported by some 22 registered patents and an additional 18 patent disclosures. My work has led to the successful introduction of 12 new products, now accounting for over $250 million in annual sales revenues.

I have extensive experience in the following specialty areas:

- Organic and Polymer Specialty Chemicals:
  - Water Treatment Chemicals
  - Oil Field and Mining Chemicals
  - Consumer Products Based on Water-

- Soluble Polymers

- Polymers, Rubbers and Plastics:
  - New Polymers and Plastics - Synthetic Approach
  - New Polymers and Plastics - Physio-Chemical Approach

My current salary is $98,000, and I have no geographical restrictions.

Should you have an appropriate opening on your research staff, Dr. Evans, I would welcome the opportunity to meet with you to discuss the contributions I might make to your new product development efforts. If interested, please contact me during evening hours at (610) 528-9375.

Thank you for your consideration, and I look forward to hearing from you.

Sincerely yours,

Kelly Marks

Kelly Marks

Enclosure

CHRISTOPHER B. HOPKINS

82 Valley View Drive   Email: CHF212@AOL.com   Office: (703) 492-2967
Anacortes, WA 22090   Home: (703) 676-3304

May 20, 2003

Mr. John B. Carver
Engineering Manager
Fulton Paper Company
33 Paper Mill Road
Winslow, ME 54952

Dear Mr. Carver:

I am interested in a position as Project Engineer with Fulton Paper Company. My resume highlights strong
project experience with Frazier Paper Company, a key competitor.

I earned a B.S. degree in Mechanical Engineering from Princeton University, and have six years of paper
machine project experience. I enjoy an excellent reputation for timely project delivery and consistent below-
budget performance. Key project experience includes:

- Completed $54 million twin-wire, forming section rebuild project
  on-time and under budget ($1.2 million savings)

- Lead Project Engineer for purchase, design and installation of wet-end section
  on new $150 million Beloit paper machine ($120,000 savings)

- Engineered, installed and started-up $45 million rebuild of after-dryer
  section of twin wire tissue machine (project completed two months ahead
  of schedule with savings of $1/2 million)

Although well-versed in most conventional machine designs, I am especially knowledgeable of twin-wire formers
and some of the newer, state-of-the-art sheet forming technology. These qualifications could prove particularly
beneficial to those companies interested in upgrading their overall papermaking technology.

If you are currently seeking a strong paper machine project engineer, I would appreciate the opportunity to
further discuss my qualifications with you. Thank you for your consideration.

Sincerely yours,

Christopher B. Hopkins

Christopher B. Hopkins

CBH/mbs

Enclosure

DIANA P. REEVES
16 Cloverdale Drive
Little Rock, AK 92805

Phone: (714) 255-3085

Email: DianaPR@MSN.com

March 16, 2005

Mr. Jeffrey A. Morse
Vice President of Human Resources
Tetra Corporation
1324 Waverly Parkway
Dallas, TX 75042

Dear Mr. Morse:

Enclosed please find my resume for a senior staffing management position at Tetra Corporation. Should you have an appropriate opening, I am confident that you will find my qualifications compelling.

My credentials include an M.S. in Industrial Relations from Arizona State University and 14 years solid human resources experience. This includes nearly nine years in the employment function (six as Manager of Administrative Employment with Emerson Electronics, Inc.), and nearly three years as a National Practice Director for Russell J. Reynolds, a premiere international executive search firm.

Additionally, I have managed a Fortune 200 employment function, including responsibility for recruitment of executive, managerial and professional employees for a wide range of business functions. I enjoy a strong reputation for cost-effective, timely, quality recruitment, and am thoroughly versed in state-of-the-art behavioral-based interviewing and assessment methodology. These skills are further complemented by strong computer skills and solid Internet recruiting expertise.

If you are seeking a knowledgeable staffing manager, please give me a call so that we may discuss your requirements.

Sincerely

Diana P. Reeves

Diana P. Reeves

DPR/jmc

Enclosure

HAROLD H. WALLACK

222 Interplex Drive
Atlanta, GA 67202
Phone: (316) 741-7255
Email: Harw88@AOL.com

July 20, 2004

Mr. Walter F. Bramson
Manager of Corporate Accounting
Brighton Chemical Company
120 Long Ridge Road
P.O. Box 1355
Newark, NJ 08923

Dear Mr. Bramson:

I am writing to apply for the position of Cost Accountant in your Corporate Accounting function. I have solid qualifications to support this application and would appreciate your consideration of the enclosed resume.

A 1997 graduate of Villanova University with a B.S. in Accounting, I have over seven years of employment in the Accounting profession. This includes four years as Auditor with Coopers & Lybrand and another three years as Cost Accountant with Burlington Industries. I have significantly benefited from excellent professional training and have consistently attained highest possible ratings during performance reviews.

Current annual compensation is $95,000, and I would anticipate a competitive offer appropriate to my qualifications and experience level.

Although open to relocation, my preference is for the mid-Atlantic region. Other locations may be of interest, however, dependent upon the specific nature of the opportunity.

If you feel that your Corporate Accounting Department could benefit from the contributions of a talented, knowledgeable Cost Accountant, I would appreciate hearing from you.

Thank you for your consideration.

Sincerely yours,

Harold H. Wallack

Harold H. Wallack

Enclosure

SHARON E. SAMUELS
145 Runyan Place
St. Louis, MO 77070

Phone: (713) 334-7933   Email: SES145@MSN.com

May 23, 2004

Mr. Bruce T. Cummins
Chief Financial Officer
Wilco Industries
635 Walker Drive, South
Cleveland OH NJ 07763

Dear Mr. Cummins:

If you are in the market for an accomplished Senior Financial Analyst with excellent reputation for successful acquisition analysis, the enclosed resume should be of interest.

My credentials include an M.B.A. in Finance from the University of Michigan and over six years acquisition analysis with the Business Development function of a Fortune 100 food company. During this period, I completed analysis of 28 acquisition candidates, resulting in acquisition of six highly profitable companies. These included:

- a $40 million acquisition of a baking company that has achieved an average ROI of 18% for the first three years of ownership

- a $28 million acquisition of a food distribution company showing a 22% ROI in the third year of operation

- a $62 million purchase of a food wrap company that yielded a 12% return during first year following acquisition

Importantly, all acquisitions have proven highly profitable, with the poorest performer achieving an ROI of 8.2%. Additionally, all acquisitions were completed at an attractive price-to-net-profit ratio.

Mr. Cummins, I would welcome the opportunity to meet with you personally to discuss the contributions I might make to Wilco Industries as a member of your Business Development staff. If you believe this a worthwhile investment, I can be reached on a confidential basis at (713) 877-9075 during business hours, or at my above home phone number during the evening.

Very truly yours,

Sharon E. Samuels

Sharon E. Samuels

Enclosure

STEPHEN S. FRAZIER

946 Cardinal Way   Email: FrazS14@MSN.com   Home: (205) 413-8996
Houston, TX 35202   Office: (205) 227-9040

November 17, 2003

Ms. Marguerite F. Courtland
Senior Vice President - Administration
Snap-On Tool Company
One Monument Square
Syracuse, NY 20355

Dear Ms. Courtland:

As the senior administrative executive of Snap-On Tool Company, perhaps you need a talented Procurement Manager who can make immediate contributions to the bottom line of your company.

As Senior Purchasing Agent for a Fortune 200, $2.8 billion, consumer products company, I enjoy a reputation as a "tough-minded negotiator," who has made significant cost-savings contributions to my employer. These have included:

- consolidated corporate-wide packaging supplies purchases with resultant annual savings of $35 million

- contributed $12 million annual savings through conversion from oil to biomass fuels with long-term purchase contract

- saved $8 million annually in inventory costs through installation of computerized raw materials tracking and forecasting system

- successfully negotiated five-year knock-down carton contract with major supplier worth $5.5 million savings annually

Educational credentials include a B.S. in Packaging from Michigan State University and an M.B.A. in Finance from Penn State University. I have more than 15 years purchasing experience with a major international corporation and have been professionally active in my field.

Compensation requirements are in the low $100,000 range, and I am open to relocation anywhere in the United States.

Should you feel my background qualifies me for a corporate procurement management opening at Snap-On Tool, I would welcome the opportunity to meet with you. Please contact me at my home in the evening.

I appreciate your consideration.

Sincerely,

Stephen S. Frazier

Stephen S. Frazier

214 Blair Mill Road
Anaheim, CA 98206

August 28, 2004

Mr. Harlan F. Martin
Director of IS
Brunswick Corporation
One North Field Court
Lenoir, NC 28633

Dear Mr. Martin:

As today's economy and competitive pressures place tighter constraints on business, IT professionals with diverse background and strong business savvy can often provide real value to their employers. I am such an individual!

As a versatile IT professional, I bring significant project management experience including exposure to a wide variety of business applications in systems and database design, quality assurance, troubleshooting and programming. Additionally, my B.B.A. in Accounting has given me an exceptional understanding of financial applications.

While at TriData, my hands-on management style and strong technical skills have enabled me to meet deadlines in high-pressured environments. I am seeking an applications management position in business systems development, or a liaison position between IT and the user community.

My current compensation is $95,000. Should you have an appropriate opening which parallels my background, I would appreciate a personal interview. I look forward to hearing from you.

Thank you for considering my credentials.

Very truly yours,

Franklin D. Jones

Franklin D. Jones

FDJ/la

Enclosure

MARY ANNE MURPHY

106 Wilson Circle   Email: MaurC@AOL.com   Home: (205) 676-4461
Mobile, AL 06484   Office: (205) 926-1801

April 16, 2005

Ms. Margaret R. Temple
Vice President of Human Resources
Cyber Communications, Inc.
1500 Irvine Blvd.
Irvine, CA 92627

Dear Ms. Temple:

I am seeking a Training and Development management position with a medium-sized technology company. A hands-on, results-oriented leader with comprehensive background in training design, development and delivery, I could be a solid addition to a company that values employee development. The enclosed resume details the specifics of my experience and accomplishments.

My background spans ten years of diverse training and development experience, providing excellent human asset development support to a variety of functional clients. In all cases I have been consistently recognized for my strong contributions and professional leadership. Client references will readily support my value to their functional organizations. The following highlights some of my key accomplishments:

- Directed training of 200 person field sales organization for major electronics distribution company

- Used assessment methodology as the basis for constructing "high performance models" for certain key management jobs. Assessed key managers against these models as the basis for defining management development needs and priorities.

- Designed and delivered company's first highly successful introductory course on statistical process control -- over 500 managers trained across 3 divisions.

- Developed methodology for linking training needs with business strategy, and implemented a reliable method for quantitatively measuring training program effectiveness.

Based on my qualifications, I am confident that I can bring effective leadership to your training function and improve the overall human resource effectiveness and productivity of your company. I would appreciate the opportunity to further discuss my credentials with you during a face-to-face interview.

I look forward to hearing from you shortly.

Yours very truly,

Mary Anne Murphy

Mary Anne Murphy

Enclosure

DANIEL R. CUNNINGHAM
240 Rosetree Trail
Chattanooga, TN 40202

October 11, 2003

Mr. William C. Collins
Vice President
Environmental Affairs Department
Matthews Chemical Company
1600 River Way
Birmingham, AL 30339

Dear Mr. Collins:

I am seeking a position where I can apply my experience as an environmental specialist. As Environmental Project Manager in Dow Chemical Company's Environmental Affairs Department, I gained considerable experience in many areas of the environmental industry, especially hazardous substance and waste management as well as environmental legislation and compliance requirements.

Specific areas of responsibility have included:

- Company compliance with applicable local, state, and federal environmental regulations nationwide

- Design and implementation of training programs to limit company risk and liability in the hazardous substance management field

- Research and evaluation of cost-effective methods for hazardous substance reduction, recycling and conservation.

I am interested in an industry position in environmental compliance, hazardous substance management, and/or industrial environmental training and education. I am also interested in a company that has a strong interest in developing pro-active programs to limit liability and reduce risks in environmental matters.

My enclosed resume further illustrates my professional competency in the environmental affairs field. Thank you for reviewing my credentials, and I look forward to hearing from you.

Sincerely,

Daniel R. Cunningham

Daniel R. Cunningham

DRC/sas

Enclosure

GEORGE T. REIKER

432 Princeton Avenue   Email: GTE902@MSN.com   Home: (502) 898-3062
Midland, MI 78229   Office: (502) 593-7100

January 15, 2003

Mr. Michael F. Johnston
Chairman of the Board
E.I. Du Pont Company
250 Main Street
Wilmington, DE 18937

Dear Mr. Johnston:

I am seeking an executive position in the chemical industry. My professional career exhibits a record of strong achievement and significant contributions as a senior member of the Dow Chemical management team. I am a top-performing chemical industry executive with an extensive, diverse management background including sales, manufacturing, research and operations.

Throughout my career, I recruited, selected and developed top management talent. I utilized persistence, technical expertise and interpersonal skills to establish and build long-term relationships with a diverse customer base. I analyzed, evaluated and led entry into new market niches enabling the company to generate significant profits, and am recognized as a creative manager with strong strategic planning, communications, listening, and operational skills. The following highlight some of my key accomplishments:

- Analyzed markets, determined special market niches, shifted product line, and aggressively led entry into new markets resulting in sales growth of 300% and a sizeable profit improvement ($520 million to $1.5 billion).

- Exercised operational P&L responsibility for a $300 million corporation, manufacturing industrial specialty O.E.M. paints and coatings.

- Landed major industrial accounts (Budd/Jeep Wrangler, Clarke Equipment, Caterpillar Trailer, Strick, and Fruehauf) by building solid relationships through persistent and creative presentations, development of superior products, and quality service.

If my qualifications are of interest, Mr. Johnston, I would be delighted to meet with you to further explore opportunities with your company. I hope we will have the opportunity to meet shortly, and I look forward to hearing from you.

Sincerely,

George T. Reiker

George T. Reiker

GTR/mas

Enclosure

MARTHA A. ROBINSON
120 Round Top Drive
Rochester, NY 21203

March 14, 2005

Mr. Robert B. Smith
Vice President IS
Parker Technologies, Inc.
1300 Technology Plaza
Boston, MA 60606

Dear Mr. Smith:

Enclosed is my resume outlining more than 15 years extensive experience in corporate telecommunications. In summary, my credentials include:

- broad experience in international computer networking

- design and implementation of voice, data, and LAN systems

- in-depth experience with telecommunications and information processing technologies

- interpersonal skills for interfacing well with all levels of management

I would like to put this expertise to work in a senior telecommunications management position and/or internal consulting role.

Although I am concentrating my search in the mid-Atlantic United States, I would consider other locations for the right opportunity.

If you are currently searching for someone with my credentials, I would be pleased to meet with you to discuss how I might contribute my technical knowledge and leadership skills in achieving your organization's strategic objectives. Thank you for your consideration.

Sincerely,

Martha A. Robinson

Martha A. Robinson

Enclosure

WILLIAM C. HARTWORTH

222 Del Mar AvenueEmail: HartWC@AOL.com   Home: (949) 966-0246
Costa Mesa, CA 39486   Office: (949) 625-3500

May 22, 2004

Ms. Carolyn B. Wilson
Director of Sales
Micro Computer Corporation
340 Irvine Blvd.
Newport Beach, CA 60173

Dear Ms. Wilson:

Are you looking for a top salesperson for the information technology industry? Maybe I can help! I am a corporate sales representative for twenty of IBM Corporation's largest customers. Based on this experience I can:

- Meet large global customers' total information systems requirements

- Negotiate worldwide volume sales agreements

- Sell in international markets

- Respond to the concerns of senior management

- Leverage all corporate resources to achieve customer satisfaction

Although other factors such as career growth are of primary importance to me, you should know that my current total compensation is in the $150,000 range.

I appreciate your consideration.

Very truly yours,

William C. Hartworth

William C. Hartworth

WCH/jos

Enclosure

608 Holly Lane
Caldwell, NJ 07000

June 22, 2004

Ms. Joan L. Garfield
Director Research & Development
Taylor Building Products Corporation
4550 State Street
McLean, VA 22102

Dear Ms. Garfield:

I am a registered engineer in the state of New Jersey, seeking a technical management position in the roofing industry. A copy of my resume is enclosed, and I would like to talk with you about career opportunities at Taylor.

In my capacity as Project Manager at CertainTeed, I am responsible for leading the development of new products for the commercial roofing industry. Part of my accountability is to provide support to sales people in fielding technical questions from engineering or architectural customers.

I also have solid experience in quality assurance and led the application of control charting methodology in the real-time process control of a large insulation product line. This effort resulted in a 23% reduction in scrap and a 76% reduction in customer complaints.

I am seeking a position as a team leader or manager in product or process development, or in quality assurance. My compensation requirements are in the $90,000 range, and I am open to relocation.

I would welcome the opportunity to talk with you and discuss the technical contributions I could make to Taylor Building Products Corporation. I have some innovative, new product ideas I think you might find quite interesting.

Thank you for reviewing my credentials, and I look forward to hearing from you shortly.

Sincerely,

Gary P. Matthews

Gary P. Matthews

Enclosure

LORETTA P. GOODWIN
2246 Sunset Avenue
East Brunswick, NJ 08816

April 16, 2004

Mr. Richard J. Purcell
Director of Quality
Cascade Electronic Corporation
One Monument Square
Syracuse, NY 13221

Dear Mr. Purcell:

I am seeking a position as a Facilitator for Total Quality Management in a firm already using TQM, or one just beginning TQM implementation.

Beginning with BS and MS degrees in engineering and following with 15 years experience with General Motors, I have built a solid foundation in shop operations, manufacturing engineering, and plant management.

Two years ago, I became convinced of the potential of Total Quality Management and began some TQM initiatives within the SUV Division. Although highly successful, due to recent budget cutbacks, many of the resources targeted for further implementation of these programs have been temporarily frozen.

I am now seeking an opportunity to continue my efforts with a company that has a firm commitment to Total Quality implementation. I have much to contribute and would welcome the opportunity to unleash my energy and enthusiasm for using TQM to drive profit to an organization's bottom line.

Should you have an appropriate opening on your quality management staff, I would appreciate the opportunity to explore employment possibilities with you. Thank you for your consideration.

Sincerely,

Loretta P. Goodwin

Loretta P. Goodwin

LPG/jmc

Enclosure

MARK G. DONNELLY

---

562 Grammercy Lane   MarkGD562@MSN.com   Home: (207) 773-6438
Portland, ME 04112   Office: (207) 834-2950

April 10, 2004

Mr. Howard T. Gross
President
Great Lakes Energy Corporation
10 West Lafayette Corporate Center
Ann Arbor, MI 48107-8600

Dear Mr. Gross:

Please take 60 seconds to consider a senior executive who has:

- Directed operations of eight international manufacturing companies with a combined sales volume of $120 million

- Increased profits by 40%, reduced late deliveries by 76% and increased market share by 15%

- As CFO, arranged debt and equity financing, implemented new manufacturing and accounting systems for a firm that grew from $18 million to $160 million in 20 months

- As a consultant, created corporate strategy for a $6 billion company

- MBA from Harvard and BS in Engineering from Princeton

- High energy, excellent interpersonal skills and experience to meet challenging opportunities such as rapid growth, business decline and turnaround situations.

Should you have room on your senior management staff for someone with my qualifications and experience, please contact me so that we can meet personally. Thank you.

Sincerely,

Mark G. Donnelly

Mark G. Donnelly

Enclosure

SYLVIA E. ARLINGTON
237 Balboa Street
Indianapolis, IN 46268

Phone: (610) 293-7753   Email: CynCar23@AOL.com

June 26, 2003

Mr. Thomas D. Barton
Vice President Operations
Carbo Beverage Company
4040 North Meridian Street
Malvern, PA 19044

Dear Mr. Barton:

I am seeking an Operations Management position at the plant, division or corporate level with a major player in the food and beverage industry. Please consider my credentials.

As my resume illustrates, I have had excellent progression in the field of Operations Management with one of the top U.S. consumer products companies. PepsiCo, as you may know, has been ranked by Fortune magazine among the top six best run companies in America.

In my current position as Group Plant Manager (three plants) for Pepsi Northeast, I have been credited with annual cost savings exceeding $2 million as the result of several innovative cost-reduction programs recently implemented. I have just been awarded Pepsi's coveted "President's Award" for my contributions.

During prior assignments I have been equally productive, consistently demonstrating the ability to achieve superior results. I pride myself on keeping current on new developments in the field of Operations and rapidly deploy new methods designed to dramatically improve operating efficiencies and reduce costs.

Should you be in the market for a proven contributor to your Operations Management Team, Mr. Barton, I believe your time would be well spent in meeting with me. Much of my learning and experience at PepsiCo are rapidly transferable to Carbo Beverage, and could result in substantial savings to your company.

Should you wish to contact me, I can be reached during the day at (610) 993-3506, or at the above number during evening hours. Thank you for your consideration.

Sincerely,

Sylvia E. Arlington

Sylvia E. Arlington

SEA/pad

Enclosure

977 Green Bay Avenue
Milwaukee, WI 53201

March 12, 2005

Mr. Vincent D. Campbell
Senior Vice President
Technology Division
Niagara Telecommunications, Inc.
180 Erie Boulevard
New York, NY 10038

Dear Mr. Campbell:

Attached is my resume. I am currently seeking a Director level position in Technical Services. My background is predominantly Telecommunications with areas of expertise in Training, Publications, and Field Service.

If you feel that my resume warrants consideration for opportunities at Niagara Telecommunications, please contact me at (414) 816-9402 or (414) 635-9576.

The enclosed resume details my background and shows a solid record of contribution and achievement. I feel an initial exploratory discussion might prove mutually beneficial.

Thank you for your time and consideration.

Sincerely,

Owen D. Johnson

Owen D. Johnson

ODJ/jes

Enclosure

BERNARD M. FOX
820 Chancellor Street
Nashville, TN 18755

May 20, 2004

Ms. Gail M. Dwyer
Director of Corporate Planning
Northrup Corporation
Electronic Systems Division
600 Hicks Road
Rolling Meadows, IL 60008

Dear Ms. Dwyer:

Do you need an accomplished professional who can provide senior management with timely, pertinent information on which to base a wide range of crucial business decisions (e.g., marketing of company products, opening of new branches, diversification of company operations, examination of the effects of new tax laws, preparation of economic forecasts)?

I hold an M.S. degree in Economics and Operations Research and am seeking a position with a growing organization that can fully challenge my research capabilities.

The enclosed resume reflects solid achievement both in the classroom and during my brief professional career. Whether in the classroom or at the workplace, I have been consistently able to meet near-term objectives while developing the tools to successfully tackle future requirements.

Excellent references can be furnished upon request.

Thank you for your time. I look forward to hearing from you.

Sincerely,

Bernard M. Fox

Bernard M. Fox

BMF/dcb

Enclosure

KIRK J. CAMERON

| 2175 Turner Lane | CamKJ@MSN.com | Home: (410) 455-9776 |
| Columbia, MD 21046 | | Office: (410) 348-6052 |

August 28, 2003

Ms. Donna M. Barnes
Director of IT
Powell Industries, Inc.
4 Penn Center Plaza, 10th Floor
Philadelphia, PA 19101

Dear Ms. Barnes:

I am seeking a position in IT management and have enclosed my resume for review against your current requirements.

My IT background includes programming, systems analysis, project management, database administration, and IT department management.

For the past seven years, I have been the IT Manager at Reliance Insurance Company in Philadelphia, responsible for planning, budgeting, organizing, and managing the daily operations of this department. In addition to supporting all end user computing on the IBM 3090 mainframe and personal computers, I am responsible for evaluating PC hardware and software, establishing PC standards and policies, consulting in the design of PC applications and maintaining both mainframe and PC security controls.

I am seeking a position in the $100,000 to $110,000 range and have no relocation restrictions.

Should you have an appropriate opening in your operations, I would appreciate the opportunity to meet with you and the members of your staff to see how my qualifications might align with your requirements. Thank you for your consideration, and I look forward to hearing from you shortly.

Very truly yours,

Kirk J. Cameron

Kirk J. Cameron

KJC/amt

Enclosure

GUY M. DeMARCO
110 Demarest Drive
Jacksonville, FL 33923

Phone: (407) 476-5012   Email: GuyDe110@MSN.com

June 10, 2003

Mr. Raymond D. Osborne
Vice President of Marketing
Hamilton Beach Corporation
1300 Cranston Street
Richmond, VA 23261

Dear Mr. Osborne:

In your efforts to continuously revitalize and strengthen your company's sales and marketing strategy, you may have a requirement for a talented, accomplished advertising executive.

My solid contributions have earned me rapid career advancement, however, I now feel a need to move on to new professional challenges.

My career covers a variety of products and services, including packaged goods, insurance, technical/industrial businesses and corporate financial/image communications. More specifically, I have:

- Developed the marketing analysis and implemented creative planning which led to improved sales of 25% for a mature, declining brand.

- In a similar role, helped maintain another brand's growth momentum with an imaginative advertising and promotion program for a line extension.

- In addition, I have strengthened and managed corporate advertising which helped change the ways in which senior business executives, consumers and the financial community perceive several major blue chip corporations.

While solving challenging marketing and customer communications problems are of primary importance to me, you should also know that my total compensation requirements are in the $95,000 to $100,000 range.

May we talk?

Sincerely,

Guy M. DeMarco

Guy M. DeMarco

GMD/tad

Enclosure

JACQUELINE E. TOYZER
412 Grant Drive
Kansas City, MO 64112

February 10, 2003

Mr. Nolan P. Kincade
President
Delcrest Corporation
1050 Bethlehem Pike
Rochester, NY 14692

Dear Mr. Kincade:

I am seeking an employment opportunity in an executive-level sales, marketing, or general management position that capitalizes on my capital goods and/or environmental background.

With over twenty years in industrial sales and marketing with Kenmore Electronics, refined with two corporate turnarounds and several start-up company assignments, I have been assisting high-tech growth firms and troubled companies in realizing their profit potential.

My consulting practice has exposed me to the environmental services sector and given me the opportunity to start-up a hospital waste disposal business and underground storage tank and ground water remediation business. I have also assisted a petroleum distributor and contractor with an aggressive growth program and a reorganized major U.S. welding equipment manufacturer with a successful acquisition/merger.

While most of my successes have been marketing focused, I would welcome the opportunity to contribute in a broader general management role that would capitalize on my entrepreneurial, marketing, and general management skills.

I will relocate (with assistance), prefer the Northeast, and will leave compensation open to negotiation.

Sincerely,

Jacqueline E. Toyzer

Jacqueline E. Toyzer

JET/hma

Enclosure

BRENT C. THURMAN
314 Centennial Drive
Smithfield, VA 23430
(804) 357-6081

May 14, 2004

Mr. Cyrus V. Moser
President
The Haagen-Dazs Company
Glenpoint Center East
Teaneck, NJ 07666

Dear Mr. Moser:

If you are seeking a top-flight Chief Financial Officer, I may well fit the bill.

In February of 1998, just after the market crash, I was successful in securing an investment grade rating on a $160 million debt for Snack Well Foods, the first time in the company's history. This was accomplished without the Canadian parent's credit support. In 2001, I successfully refinanced $110 million of acquisition debt for a U.S. subsidiary of Hostess Foods. It allowed them to sell the company for a premium.

During my tenure as senior or chief financial officer with past employers, I have developed several new credit facilities through both private and public sources. In some cases, these have been quite unique. For instance, the first insured, unleveraged multi-property real estate investment deal for the food franchising industry was masterminded by me. This business has grown to over $3.6 billion of assets now under management. I have employed captive lending facilities to improve investor returns as well as tax-advantaged concepts like money market preferred stock. Of course, more traditional means like commercial paper and direct bank borrowing have been sourced as well.

I have a diverse business background with successful experience in manufacturing, distribution, financial services and retail. For nineteen years, cash flow improvement (whether through financing, cost containment/reduction, or revenue enhancement) has consistently resulted from my efforts.

Although more interested in a challenging opportunity with an interesting company than merely making money, you should know that in recent years my total compensation has been in the $175,000 to $200,000 range.

Should you be seeking a senior financial officer with my credentials, Mr. Moser, I would appreciate the chance to meet with you. Thank you for your consideration.

Sincerely,

Brent C. Thurman

Brent C. Thurman

Enclosure

33

KATHLEEN B. SCHEIGH

1018 Fairview Knoll	Email: KB Scheigh@ AOL.com	Home: (316) 229-8044
Brook Park, OH 44142	Cell: (316) 278-9047	Office: (316) 984-0720

July 10, 2002

Mr. Charles D. Pemberton
Director of Procurement
Allstar Plastics, Inc.
3041 Skyway Circle
Irving, TX 7538

Dear Mr. Pemberton:

I have six years of increasing responsibility as a Procurement professional, including two years as a manager reporting to the Division Manager of Sebastian Company's hair-care products business. A sampling of some of my key accomplishments includes:

- Saved $800,000 in raw materials costs in ten months for an established brand through supplier contract re-negotiations.

- Consolidated purchasing for poly wrap and negotiated national contract producing over $1.2 million annual savings.

- Installed JIT computer system cutting spare parts inventory requirements and saving $1/2 million annually in inventory investment.

- Initiated changes in folding carton specification that increased packaging functionality and cut vital supplies inventory investment by $220,000 annually.

The enclosed resume will provide you with further examples of other major contributions that I have made. Perhaps Allstar Plastics may also wish to benefit from my creativity and energy. If so, I can be reached at any of the phone numbers listed above.

I hope that we will have the opportunity to discuss my qualifications further during a personal meeting. Thank you for your consideration.

Very truly yours,

Kathleen B. Scheigh

Kathleen B. Scheigh

Enclosure

810 Farnam Street
Greenville, SC 29602

September 16, 2004

Mr. Christopher B. Reese
Director of Employment
Mosinee Paper Company
11830 Westline Industrial Park
Mosinee, W I54455-9099

Dear Mr. Reese:

I have been employed with Bowater Paper & Pulp Group for the last three years and have decided to make a change. I am originally from the Milwaukee area and would like the opportunity to return to Wisconsin.

I noted Mosinee Paper was undergoing considerable expansion, with plans to add three plants and a research center over the next three years. This suggests that you will need to recruit the technical and operations personnel to staff these new facilities. Perhaps I can help.

I hold a B.A. degree in Business from Western Michigan University and have three years of experience as Technical Employment Manager with Bowater Paper & Pulp. As such, I am responsible for all technical and operations staffing for the company, including the Technology Center and six manufacturing plants. During the last two years alone, I have recruited and successfully filled 150 technical and operations professional and managerial positions.

Some key accomplishments include:

- Staffed over 200 professional and managerial positions in three years

- Reduced employee turnover by 30% through implementation of improved interviewing and selection techniques

- Reduced interview-to-hire ratio by 28%, saving over $50,000 per year in candidate travel expenses

- Reduced recruiting time by 50% through implementation of creative recruiting strategies

If you will need an experienced employment professional who has first-hand knowledge of technical and operations recruiting in the paper industry, you may want to give me a call. I am sure that I can provide the kind of recruiting support that will be required by Mosinec Paper to successfully meet its staffing requirements and achieve its expansion objectives.

Thank you for your consideration.

Sincerely,

J. Robert Sweeney

J. Robert Sweeney

Enclosure

BETH A. FURGESON

622 Appleford Lane
Scranton, PA 17652

FergBA@AOL.com

Office: (717) 576-3116
Home: (717) 944-4081

February 18, 2003

Mr. Leonard S. Weinstein
Vice President Marketing
Tri-State Property Development
One Liberty Place, 36th Floor
New York, NY 10221

Dear Mr. Weinstein:

I am seeking a challenging real estate, business development, sales and marketing position with an organization that can benefit from my knowledge and skills. During my career I have accumulated a record of solid achievement and significant contribution. The enclosed resume details both my experience and these accomplishments.

During four years of successful business development and sales and marketing experience, I have continuously been singled out for my creativity and ability to identify and implement highly profitable projects. The following highlights some of my achievements:

- Arranged financing to cover acquisition and development costs (and prepared all necessary pro forma and cash flow analysis) for a $6 million commercial development project

- Implemented successful sales and marketing plan to establish a strong market presence for a Central Pennsylvania office of a Philadelphia-based development company

- Sold over $22 million in aggregate real estate leaseholds (56) during first 24 months (over 5 million square feet of commercial/industrial real estate)

- Obtained all necessary approvals for a 300-unit residential subdivision

If my qualifications are of interest to you, I would welcome the chance to meet with you personally and further explore career opportunities at Tri-State Property Development. Thank you for considering my qualifications.

Sincerely,

Beth A. Furgeson

Beth A. Furgeson

Enclosure

KEITH R. COLLINS, Ph.D.

670 Union Street
Monroe, GA 30655

February 12, 2005

Dr. Alfred J. Lloyd
Director Research & Development
Armor-All Products Corporation
Six Westside Avenue
Upland, IN 46989

Dear Dr. Lloyd:

I am seeking a challenging position as a chemist in the paints and coatings, chemical, petroleum, or rubber industry. My interests, education, and experience specifically qualify me for a challenging technical assignment in product development, quality control, chemical safety, and/or hazardous substances handling.

My innovation and related career success have centered around formulation, characterization, and physical testing of polymer coatings, elastomers, and fibers. My knowledge of many laboratory instruments, experience in customer service, public speaking, and technical presentations should prove valuable assets.

After you have reviewed my resume, I would appreciate the opportunity to discuss my credentials and how I might contribute to Armor-All Products and its technical objectives.

Thank you.

Sincerely,

Keith R. Collins

Keith R. Collins

KRC/dan

Enclosure

NORMAN A. CARTWRIGHT

176 Breezewood Estates, Sacramento, CA 95814

April 26, 2004

Mr. Wayne A. Higgins
Director of Marketing
Precision Instruments, Inc.
1920 Fifth Street
Davis, CA 95616

Dear Mr. Higgins:

Your review of my enclosed resume will be appreciated.

Briefly, I am a senior sales representative with broad program management experience and a technical background in process control and measurement as applied to production, transmission, and distribution of electricity and various industrial processes.

Should you have a suitable requirement that is appropriate to my experience, please contact me by phone at (916) 442-1733. I would be pleased to meet with you at your convenience.

Very truly yours,

Norman A. Cartwright

Norman A. Cartwright

Enclosure

ANGELO S. MARUCCI
212 Piccolo Street
Petersburg, VA 23219
(804) 487-9167

April 20, 2005

Mr. William J. Cumberland
Regional Sales Manager
Font Master Software Inc.
2000 South Central Boulevard
Virginia Beach, VA 23454

Dear Mr. Cumberland:

As the Regional Sales Manager for one of America's premiere software companies, I am sure you are always on the lookout for outstanding sales talent. Should your region, or another Font Master sales region, be in the market for a proven sales leader with an excellent record of achievement, you may want to give me a call.

My qualifications include a B.A. in Marketing from Ohio State and four years in technical sales with Crown Data Corporation in the East Coast region. Some highlights of my career include:

- Doubled territory sales volume in four years ($2 to $4 million).

- Increased new accounts from 350 to over 700.

- Won annual regional sales contest two years in a row.

My full resume is enclosed for your reference.

I feel that career growth opportunities at Crown Data are somewhat limited, and I have made a decision to seek a sales position with a more progressive company offering greater opportunity for upward mobility. Compensation requirements are in the $85,000 to $95,000 range plus company automobile and expenses.

If you feel my credentials are of interest, I would welcome a call and the opportunity to interview with your firm. I can normally be reached at my home after 7:00 p.m.

Thank you for your consideration.

Sincerely,

Angelo S. Marucci

Angelo S. Marucci

Enclosure

MARTHA D. ADAMSON
576 Glenside Avenue
Des Moines, IA 50313

Home: (515) 262-3406   *Cell*: (437) 998-774   *Email*: Mara57@MSN.com

July 22, 2002

Mr. Noel G. Franks
Director of Manufacturing
Scientific Glass Products, Inc.
Beeker Street
Windom, MN 56101

Dear Mr. Franks:

I wish to explore career opportunities in operations management with Scientific Glass Products and am enclosing my resume for your consideration. Should you be in the market for an energetic, results-oriented manufacturing manager for one of your plants, I would encourage you to consider my credentials.

A 1997 graduate of Iowa State University with a B.S. degree in Industrial Engineering, I have five years' manufacturing experience in the glass industry with Wheaton Glass. During this time, I advanced from Shift Supervisor - Furnace Operations to Operations Manager of a 400-employee pharmaceutical glass manufacturing facility.

Some of my major contributions include:

- Successful installation and start-up of a $25 million glass manufacturing line (on time & under budget)

- Automation of packaging department resulting in 30% reduction in labor costs ($4 million annual savings)

- Redesign of work assignments for finishing department and initiation of skills training, resulting in 20% productivity increase

My strong contributions in manufacturing, coupled with solid knowledge of glass manufacturing operations, should make me an attractive candidate for an operations management assignment with your company. Should you agree, I would welcome the opportunity to meet with you and further explore this possibility.

Thank you for considering my qualifications, and I look forward to hearing from you.

Sincerely,

Martha D. Adamson

Martha D. Adamson

Enclosure

ARTHUR D. BOWES

240 Mockingbird Lane, Cass City, MI 48726   *Phone: (415)876-2476*

February 24, 2003

Mr. Lawrence S. Solomon
Director of Logistics
Vulcan Oil Corporation
1818 Metroplex Drive
Dallas, TX 75265-5907

Dear Mr. Solomon:

As Director of Logistics for a major oil company, I'm sure you are keenly aware of the financial contributions that a skilled Distribution Manager can make to the corporate bottom line. It is for this reason you may wish to pay particular attention to my employment qualifications as highlighted on the enclosed resume.

My credentials include a B.A. degree in Business Administration from the University of Michigan and over 15 years' experience in distribution and distribution management in the chemical process and petrochemical industry. I am currently Distribution Manager for the Lubes Division of Pennzoil Corporation.

Selected accomplishments include:

- Implemented regional warehousing concept, consolidating 12 warehouses into five regional centers ($8 million annual savings).

- Automated three regional warehouses allowing for unitized handling of finished product and reduction of product damage by 60% (annual savings of $2 million).

- Negotiated national truck fleet maintenance contract, reducing maintenance costs by 20% ($1.8 million annual savings).

I am seeking a senior position in distribution management at either the corporate or division level. Compensation requirements are in the $95,000 to $100,000 range.

Should you have an appropriate management opening, I would welcome the opportunity to meet with you personally to explore the contributions that I could make to your distribution operations.

Thank you for your review of my qualifications, and I look forward to your reply.

Sincerely,

Arthur D. Bowes

Arthur D. Bowes

Enclosure

MONICA C. HEINTZ

| 901 St. John's Drive | MonHein@AOL.com | Home: (603) 334-6521 |
| Hampton, NH 03842 | Cell: (603) 556-9038 | Office: (603) 929-4700 |

August 26, 1998

Mr. Kenneth J. Schroeder
Director of Engineering
Groundwater Technologies
405 Frontier Plaza
Danbury, CT 06833

Dear Mr. Schroeder:

Preliminary research of your company indicates that your firm is engaged in handling large-scale engineering and start-up projects in the waste treatment field. In particular, I am quite interested in the work that you are doing in the area of site remediation. This is a field in which I have expertise.

As the enclosed resume will demonstrate, I am a degreed engineer with some ten years' experience in project engineering management of large-scale site remediation projects. During the past four years, in fact, I have been Site Remediation Engineering Manager for the Roy F. Weston Company and have directed some of Weston's largest projects for the Environmental Protection Agency.

I am thoroughly versed in all aspects of site remediation including site evaluation and analysis as well as on-site management of the remediation process itself. I am also familiar with a wide range of remediation technologies including low- and high-temperature thermal treatment systems.

In addition to my project management expertise, I am considered a key resource to the marketing group in the sale of Weston engineering and consulting services in the site remediation area. I have played a key role in helping to land over $85 million in site remediation engineering projects in the past two years alone.

If you are in the market for a strong engineering manager to direct and grow your site remediation business, perhaps you might want to give me a call. I have the technical, marketing and managerial expertise necessary to profitably lead a major expansion of this segment of your business and place you in a highly competitive position in this dynamic, fast-growing market.

Thank you for your consideration, and I look forward to hearing from you shortly.

Sincerely

Monica C. Heintz

Monica C. Heintz

Enclosure

330 Palomino Drive
Louisville, KY 40218

March 16, 2003

Ms. Sharon A. McBryde
Creative Director
VIP Advertising
1650 Pacific Highway
Carmel, CA 90393

Dear Ms. McBryde:

Creativity is the lifeblood of the advertising profession and the core value that separates the elite agency from the mundane and boring. My clients have been anything but bored, and their advertising-driven sales revenue increases have generated more than a mild interest in what I have to offer.

Unfortunately, although my current employer enjoys a healthy cash flow generated by my creative contributions to the firm, the agency is a small family-owned operation and there appears to be little opportunity for career growth beyond my current position. This has forced me to consider other career alternatives.

Please accept my resume in application for a management position on your creative department's staff. I am seeking the opportunity to manage a small group in the development of creative ideas for T.V. commercials and national print media advertising campaigns. Compensation requirements are in the $100,000 range.

My portfolio is replete with award-winning, sales-getting advertising campaigns for such major companies as Westinghouse, Procter & Gamble, Campbell Soup, Johnson & Johnson, and others. Through the use of my creative talents, my employer has both landed and expanded business with these key firms, with sales revenues now valued at approximately $150 million annually.

Perhaps we should meet to explore how I might put my creative energies to work for your agency. Should you agree, please contact me at my home number during week nights after 8:00 p.m.

Thank you for your consideration.

Very truly yours,

Regina D. Lennox

Regina D. Lennox

Enclosure

Elizabeth A. Larkin

741 Rambling Way
Phoenix, AZ 85023

Email: LizLar@MSN.com

Res: (602) 484-0332
Bus: (602) 693-0800

July 12, 2004

Mr. Warren S. Dithers
Director of Procurement
Coordinated Apparel, Inc.
5760 West 96th Street
Los Angeles, CA 90040

Dear Mr. Dithers:

Enclosed please find my resume in application for the position of Senior Buyer with your firm.   Review of my credentials will confirm that I am a skilled, hard-working procurement professional with a propensity for continuous improvement and a real knack for delivering profit to the bottom line.

Some noteworthy contributions include:

- Consolidated corporate-wide purchases of primary chemicals resulting in volume discount and $5 million annual savings.

- Initiated blanket order system with five-hour guaranteed delivery of key packaging materials, reducing raw material inventory by 74% and resulting in $1.6 million annual savings.

- Secured 10% price reduction in purchase of all rayon fiber from major supplier (annual savings of $1.1 million).

I feel confident that I can bring similar cost savings to Coordinated Apparel as well.

My qualifications include a B.S. degree in Chemistry from the University of Southern California and six years of highly successful raw materials and packaging procurement for a well-known manufacturer of nonwoven fabrics.   I have been continuously recognized by my employer for outstanding performance and can furnish excellent references upon request.

Should you have a need for a strong procurement professional, I trust you will give me a call. Thank you for considering my credentials, and I look forward to your reply.

Sincerely,

Elizabeth A. Larkin

Elizabeth A. Larkin

Enclosure

PAUL C. GIFFORD
909 Allendale Avenue
Springford, Pennsylvania 19803
(215) 655-9153

September 23, 2003

Mr. Stanley D. Humphries
Manager of IS
Hercules, Inc.
Market Street Towers, East
Philadelphia, PA 19102

Dear Mr. Humphries:

I heard some rumors through industry contacts that Hercules is considering installation of a computerized MRP system throughout its Specialty Products Division. If you are looking for a project leader or senior systems analyst for this project, I would be an ideal candidate.

My credentials include a B.S. in Computer Science from Drexel University and over 10 years as a systems analyst with Titan Chemical Company in Cherry Hill. Titan, as you are likely aware, is a $560 million manufacturer of specialty chemicals sold to the agricultural chemicals industry. Currently, I hold the position of Senior Systems Analyst.

Of particular interest should be the fact that I have spent the last two years as the lead systems analyst in the installation and successful start-up of a computerized MRP system at Titan. This project was highly successful and was completed ahead of time and on budget.

The Vice President of Manufacturing has stated that this was the most successful system installation that he has ever witnessed at Titan. The start-up was practically flawless, and the transition from manual system to computer was accomplished without missing a beat. The success of this project resulted in my receipt of a $10,000 special bonus in recognition of my contribution as the lead systems analyst.

I am enclosing a copy of my resume so that you might become familiar with the specifics of my qualifications and experience.

Should you have an interest in pursuing my candidacy, I would be pleased to hear from you. I can be reached at my home most evenings between the hours of 7:30 and 10:00 p.m.

Thank you for your consideration.

Sincerely,

Paul C. Gifford

Paul C. Gifford

Enclosure

3

Letters to Search Firms

Search firms and employment agencies are important sources for use in the job search. Surveys show that these firms account for some 10 to 15% of all professional and managerial jobs found by the job seeker. These studies also demonstrate that such organizations are the second most productive source; only networking (personal contact) is more successful. These facts should be remembered when planning your job-hunting campaign.

In designing your job search, therefore, you will want to target search firms and/or employment agencies as a key source of jobs. Since most of these firms will not accept unsolicited telephone calls from job seekers, it is impractical to think of maximizing the use of this job source by using the telephone or by simply walking in the door unexpectedly. This leaves only one practical means for accessing these firms—use of a direct-mail campaign.

My firm, Brandywine Consulting Group, has experimented with the use of direct mail to these third-party agencies as a job search method. As with direct-mail campaigns to the employer, our experience shows that, on any given mailing, between 3 to 5% of these third-party agencies respond with an interest in the candidate. These statistics seem to hold true for professional through upper-middle-management level positions. There is, however, a significant drop-off in response rate for persons in senior executive positions (that is, those at the top 5% of executive earnings levels).

If you are at the professional through upper-middle management level, it is probably worth your while to use a mass-mail approach to contact these firms. In fact, even senior level executives will want to consider using this technique. However, they should not have unrealistic expectations concerning the number of positive responses they will receive. Mailing to 500 or 600 search firms/employment agencies should generally yield 15 to 30 favorable responses. In other words, approximately 15 to 30 of these firms will typically call to discuss a particular opportunity with one of their clients.

In one Brandywine Consulting Group mailing to some 800 companies, for example, the candidate received 24 calls. These calls resulted in 8 job interviews and 3 offers of employment. All of this activity occurred within 37 work days of the start of the candidate's job search program.

This example clearly demonstrates that the direct-mail campaign, aimed at search firms and employment agencies, can sometimes prove to be a very powerful job-search technique. A good broadcast cover letter can greatly impact the success of this particular job-hunting method.

COVER LETTER PURPOSE

The type of broadcast cover letter employed in making a third-party agency mailing is somewhat different from that used in a similar mailing to employers. The difference has to do with the particular roles of these firms.

The employer is motivated to find uniquely qualified individuals who can "add value" to their organization. As a result, the employer may tend to read the cover letter more thoroughly than the search firm or employment agency, possibly also considering the candidate's qualifications for more than one opening.

By contrast, the search firm or employment agency's role is to match the candidate's qualifications with the requirements of the specific position covered by their search agreement with the employer. Rather than looking at the candidate's broader qualifications as presented in the cover letter, most agencies will skip the cover letter entirely and go straight to the resume.

Search firms and employment agencies have long realized that the cover letter is often somewhat redundant to the resume, frequently containing much of the same information. Further, unnecessarily reading cover letters can easily add 30% to 50% to the recruiter's workload, making him or her far less productive and efficient. Why, then, waste time reading cover letters if the resume is the more complete document for evaluating a candidate against the client's requirements? Consequently, many third-party agencies will read the cover letter only after they have first scanned the resume and determined that an appropriate match exists. At this point, however, they will carefully read the cover letter for other clues about the candidate's overall qualifications.

Most third-party agencies view the cover letter principally as a "transmittal letter." This means they view its primary purpose as simply serving as the vehicle for transmitting the candidate's resume. Thus, there is reduced likelihood that the job seeker can use the cover letter to make the initial sale. In such cases, therefore, it is imperative that a well-written resume document accompany the cover letter.

KEY LETTER ELEMENTS

Since the principal purpose of the third-party agency cover letter is *resume transmittal*, these letters tend to be relatively brief when compared to the broadcast letters used with employers. The principal difference between the two is that the search firm/employment agency letter places less emphasis on selling specific value and more emphasis on providing a general, overall summary of qualifications.

The following are key elements normally found in the third-party agency broadcast cover letter:

1. First paragraph contains:
   - Statement of job search objective (position sought)
   - Request to be considered for firm's current and future job search assignments
2. Second paragraph contains an overall "qualifications summary" including:
   - Educational credentials
   - Relevant work experience
3. Third paragraph normally contains a "statement of appreciation" for the firm's review and consideration of the applicant's qualifications.

In addition to using these "standard" paragraphs, authors of these types of cover letters may choose to include one or more of the following optional paragraphs:

1. Explanation of reason for making career change.
2. A "selling" or "value-adding" paragraph citing key accomplishments relevant to job search objective.
3. A statement specifying compensation requirements.
4. A statement specifying geographical preferences or restrictions.
5. A statement providing contact instructions.

The balance of this chapter provides a wide selection of well-written third-party agency cover letters that should facilitate your design of an effective letter for use in your own job-hunting campaign.

GREGORY A. NORTON

7 Michigan Avenue, Dundee, Illinois 60118   *Phone: (715) 478-2947*

June 18, 2003

Mr. Peter J. Gavin
The Northland Agency
5667 Fritztown Road
Minneapolis, MN 55426

Dear Mr. Gavin:

I understand from some of my associates that your agency specializes in placing technical personnel in the electronics field. Perhaps you are currently working on an assignment for one of your clients which might align well with my qualifications and requirements.

I am seeking a position as a Programmer Analyst providing technical programming support to Development Engineers in the development of state-of-the-art communications controllers or related technology. Key qualifications include:

- M.S. degree in Computer Science

- Three years technical programming support experience in an R&D electronics environment

- In-depth knowledge of the SNA/ACP/NCP functions of a communications controller in a PEP environment

- Proficiency in SNA/ACP/NCP internals

- Proficiency with SDLC, various trace facilities, ALC and TSO/WYLBUR/SPF

- Expert in use of data analyzer equipment

My current compensation is $75,000 and I have no geographical restrictions.

Should you be aware of a suitable opportunity, I would appreciate hearing from you. Thank you for your consideration.

Sincerely,

Gregory A. Norton

Gregory A. Norton

Enclosure

WILLIAM A. BARLOW
1622 Poinsettia Street
Richmond, VA 29202-1752

March 30, 2004

Mr. Ronald L. Wise
Management Recruiters, Inc.
30 Woodstock Street
Roswell, GA 30075

Dear Mr. Wise:

Could one of your client companies use an ambitious, energetic accounting professional, with an excellent record of growth and accomplishment, as an accounting supervisor?

I am thoroughly trained and ready for my first supervisory assignment. I have a solid technical foundation in accounting fundamentals, which I gained during my last three years of employment at Precision Electronics, Inc. In addition, I have strong interpersonal, communications and leadership skills, which should serve me well in a supervisory role.

Beyond my professional experience, I hold both a B.A. and M.B.A. from Syracuse University, where I majored in accounting. As my resume will attest, I was both a scholar and a campus leader.

Although I would prefer to remain in the Eastern U.S., I will give serious consideration to other locations, should the opportunity warrant.

Should you identify a suitable opportunity for me, Mr. Wise, I can be reached on a confidential basis at my office during the day or at my home during evening hours. Both phone numbers are on the enclosed resume.

Thank you.

Sincerely,

William A. Barlow

William A. Barlow

Enclosure

THOMAS C. WOOD

1808 Skyline Drive   Home: (412) 977-8104
Pittsburgh, PA 14332   Office:(412) 323-4076

July 22, 2003

Mr. Willard B. Travis
Travis & Co., Inc.
325 Boston Post Road
Sudbury, MA 01776

Dear Mr. Travis:

For the past several years, I have been running the Chemicals Division of General Industries, Inc. In May of this year, that business was sold to Dow Chemical Company and, as a result, I am now in the process of contemplating a possible career change.

I understand that your company services the chemical industry and I thus decided to forward a copy of my resume for your review.

If you know of any suitable opportunities, I would appreciate hearing from you. Should you require additional information, or need to discuss my qualifications in greater detail, please give me a call. Thank you for your consideration.

                                        Sincerely,

                                        Thomas C. Wood

                                        Thomas C. Wood

TCW/dn

Enclosure

FAYE M. ANDERSON
133 Sheffield Avenue
Inverness, FL 32650
(814) 357-9018

October 10, 2003

Mr. George L. Resinger
Sigma Group, Inc.
600 17th Street, Ste. 1440
Brentwood, TN 37207

Dear Mr. Resinger:

I am seeking a project engineering position in the metals industry. My research indicates your firm services clients in the metals and related industries, so I am enclosing my resume for your review and consideration.

I am an ambitious, motivated Senior Project Engineer with five years experience in the design, installation and start-up of aluminum manufacturing processes and equipment. I have strong engineering skills and have earned an excellent reputation for project timeliness and cost efficiency. The following are some of my key accomplishments:

- Managed mechanical design of $20 million aluminum furnace complex (completed on time and under budget.)

- Redesigned refractory lining in a flash calciner process to reduce heat loss by 30% in existing units and 50% in new units. (Potential savings $4.5 million annually.)

- Directed design and installation of $12 million furnace and associated material handling equipment. (Completed two months ahead of schedule and 15% under budget.)

Should one of your client companies be in search of a results-oriented, highly motivated senior project engineer with my credentials, I would appreciate the opportunity to further discuss my qualifications with you.

My geographical preference is in the Southwestern United States, and my compensation requirements are in the low $70,000 range.

Thank you for your consideration, and I look forward to hearing from you.

Very truly yours,

Faye M. Anderson

Faye M. Anderson

Enclosure

DENNIS M. RUSSELL

1427 Alberta Drive   **Email: *RussDM@AOL.com***   *Home: (316) 898-4051*
Cleveland, OH 44115   *Office: (316) 477-9161*

September 12, 2003

Ms. Kathleen O'Callaghan
O'Callaghan & Associates Inc.
1127 Euclid Avenue, Suite 375
Ft. Worth, TX 76109

Dear Ms. O'Callaghan:

I am writing to inquire about career opportunities that may exist within your client community.

I am currently Director of Systems Development with Computer World Stores in Cleveland, Ohio, and was previously with the Information Services Division of Carter Hawley Hale Stores in Anaheim, California.

I have in excess of 20 years of experience in retail systems development within the IS organizations, which includes major accomplishments in systems development, data administration, data center computer operations, information center and quality assurance departments.

Although I'm far more interested in finding a good company and an interesting opportunity, you should be aware that my annual compensation has been in the $125,000 to $130,000 range during the last few years.

I look forward to the opportunity to more fully describe my credentials, should you have a suitable assignment for which I qualify. Thank you.

Sincerely,

Dennis M. Russell

Dennis M. Russell

Enclosure

FRANCIS J. MADDEN

610 Newport Drive, Hampden, Maine 04644

May 12, 2003

Mr. Robert C. Grecco
Grecco, Divine & Co., Inc.
4100 International Plaza
Tower II, Suite 600
New York, NY 10017

Dear Mr. Grecco:

I am writing in anticipation that you may be seeking talented claims management or operations professionals for one of your insurance industry clients. With a consistent track record of success in both the property and casualty and managed healthcare industries, I believe I could immediately contribute to a variety of claims and operational issues.

I have enclosed my resume to provide an overview of my qualifications and would be pleased to discuss my career goals in greater detail during an exploratory conversation.

Should you have employment opportunities which you feel may be of interest to me, I would appreciate hearing from you. My home phone number is (207) 848-5693.

Thank you for your consideration, and I look forward to hearing from you.

Sincerely,

Francis J. Madden

Francis J. Madden

Enclosure

April 14, 2003

Ms. Judith T. McCall
McCall Resources
1511 Sansome Street, 21st Floor
San Francisco, CA 94104

Dear Ms. McCall:

Enclosed please find my resume for your review and consideration against either current or future search assignments in the Human Resources field.

I am seeking a responsible, challenging corporate or division level position as a human resource generalist. Consideration would also be given to a position in the field of Labor Relations.

My salary requirements are in the $85,000 range with flexibility dependent upon geographic area, future opportunity and similar considerations. Although I have no absolute geographical restrictions, I do have a strong preference for the West and Southwest regions.

Thank you for your consideration, and I look forward to the prospect of discussing appropriate career opportunities with you or a member of your staff.

Sincerely,

Karen E. Ashby

Karen E. Ashby

KEA:seb

Enclosure

FREDERICK A. LIVINGSTON

2110 Alabaster Avenue
Lapeer, MI 48446   Email: Fliv2110@MSN.com   Home: (603) 227-6113
                                                                               Office: (603) 762-6318

May 25, 2004

Mr. Lee Koehn
Lee Koehn Associates, Inc.
250 Route 28, Suite 206
Bridgewater, NJ 08807

Dear Mr. Koehn:

I am seeking challenging opportunities in Operations Management at the corporate, division, or major operating level. Perhaps one of your current or future clients may be looking for a strong Operations Executive and have an interest in my qualifications.

As my resume shows, I have had excellent career progression in the field of Operations Management at both DuPont and Dow Chemical Company. Unfortunately, my division has been sold and my position as Director of Operations has been eliminated.

You will note I have established an excellent track record for generating overall cost reduction and operating efficiency gains for each of my past employers. I take particular pride in staying current with new approaches and methodologies, and am quick to apply those that generate solid bottom line results.

If one of your clients seeks a motivated Operations Executive with strong leadership skills and a demonstrated record for running efficient and profitable operations, I would encourage you to consider me.

I can be reached, during the day or evening, at the numbers listed on this letterhead.

Very truly yours,

Frederick A. Livingston

Frederick A. Livingston

FAL/pl

Enclosure

ROSE MARIE DOYLE

501 Cambridge Street   Email: *RMDoyle@MSN.com*   *Home: (617) 676-3150*
Boston, MA 02141   *Office: (617) 297-6363*

December 3, 2002

Mr. David R. Biren
Senior Partner
The Biren Agency, Inc.
14 South Park Street
Montclair, NJ 07042

Dear Mr. Biren:

I am a results-oriented, senior-level marketing executive with over 14 years experience in all phases of marketing and sales management. Innovativeness is my greatest asset, and I am credited with substantial increases in overall sales volume resulting from fresh market approaches and creative ideas I contributed to employers.

The following are key accomplishments:

- Catapulted company to Number 1 in European specialty resins market in only two years (33% increase in export sales)

- Led national roll-out of low-viscosity resin product with resultant $58 million sales in first year

- Repositioned old brand, through creative advertising approach, that revitalized product and resulted in 150% increase in sales volume in six months

- Replaced independent manufacturers representative network with direct sales force, reducing cost-of-sales 30% over three-year period

- Directed installation of order-tracking computer system that led to 23% reduction in order delivery time in 18 months.

The enclosed resume further details my extensive experience and qualifications.

Should one of your specialty chemical industry clients be in the market for a top-flight marketing and sales executive to join their senior management team, perhaps you will give my qualifications serious consideration. My knowledge, creativity and energy could prove a valuable asset in helping them realize their full market potential.

Thank you for your consideration.

Sincerely,

Rose Marie Doyle

Rose Marie Doyle

Enclosure

233 Westheimer Lane
Norwalk, CT 06854

July 5, 2003

Ms. Brenda C. Hawkins
The Hawkins Group
2340 Orrington Avenue
Portland, ME 20116

Dear Ms. Hawkins:

I am a senior human resources executive with over 15 years experience and am currently Director of Corporate Staff Human Resources for Hanson Paper Company, a $5.5 billion, Fortune 200 consumer products company.

Although Hanson has treated me well, I have some concerns about future career progression in light of planned consolidation of the corporate staff organization. This consolidation, coupled with the relatively young age of the company's current top human resource executive group, suggests future career advancement to senior levels will be severely limited. I have thus opted to confidentially explore career options elsewhere.

My qualifications include an M.B.A. from Michigan State University, with emphasis in Human Resource Management. My career progression at Hanson has included human resource management assignments at the corporate, division, and manufacturing plant level. I am well schooled and heavily experienced in a wide range of human resource functions, including: organization design, management development, staffing, compensation and benefits, and labor relations.

I am seeking a senior human resources position at the vice-presidential level, with full responsibility for all human resource functions. Compensation requirements are in the $150,000 plus range, and I am open to relocation to most parts of the United States.

Should one of your clients be in the market for a senior-level human resources executive with my credentials, I would appreciate a call. Thank you for your consideration.

Sincerely,

Vincent J. Hartman

Vincent J. Hartman

Enclosure

WALLACE D. POLK, Ph.D.

510 Monroe Street
Evanston, IL 60201
(312) 437-9736

January 13, 2003

Mr. Stephen Goldram
Stephen Goldram Search Consultants, Inc.
P. O. Box 33
Gary, IL 60013

Dear Mr. Goldram:

I am a PhD organic chemist from Columbia University with 12 years of experience in R&D and R&D management, and also hold an MBA with three years experience in business development and analysis including acquisitions, foreign joint ventures, and strategic planning.

My areas of technical expertise are polymer composites, adhesives, polymer chemistry in unsaturated polyester, vinyl ester, urethane and epoxy, fine organic chemicals, petrochemicals, and homogeneous and heterogeneous catalysis.

I am capable of handling a wide spectrum of business development projects ranging from new application/product development and new market development, to creating entirely new businesses, to strategic expansion via acquisition and joint venture.

I am seeking a management position in a technology-oriented polymer chemical company in business/market development or research and development, where I can fully utilize both my technical and business expertise to create new business opportunities for my employer.

I am willing to relocate and would consider positions paying in excess of $110,000 per year.

If you are aware of a suitable employment opportunity with one of your clients, I would appreciate hearing from you. Thank you.

Yours very truly,

Wallace D. Polk

Wallace D. Polk

Enclosure

ELAINE D. HOFFMEIR

1549 Chelsea Court
Beachwood, OH 44122

Home: (614) 745-4372
Office: (614) 997-0300

April 26, 2005

Mr. John T. Erlanger
Erlanger Associates
2 Pickwick Plaza
Greenwich, CT 06830

Dear Mr. Erlanger:

Your clients may be in search of a Total Quality Manager who has successfully led the implementation of an SPC-based total quality effort on a company-wide basis. I have successfully led such an effort. Enclosed is my resume which provides specifics of my qualifications.

OBJECTIVE:	Corporate Manager - Total Quality
LOCATION:	Northeastern United States
COMPENSATION:	$90,000 to $100,000
TRAVEL:	Up to 60% Acceptable

Should you require further information, I can be reached at the phone numbers listed above.

Thank you.

Sincerely,

Elaine D. Hoffmeir

Elaine D. Hoffmeir

Enclosure

EUGENE A. DROMESHAUSER

1014 Old Forest Lane, Broomall, PA 19008   *Phone: (610) 337-5619*

April 23, 2002

Ms. Linda E. Brolin
LEB Associates, Inc.
124 N. Summit Street, Suite 3305
Toledo, OH 43604

Dear Ms. Brolin:

Although I enjoy the challenges of my present position, I am seeking alternatives to a lengthy commute into New York City. Perhaps one of your clients may have a requirement for a procurement professional with strong background in the purchase of packaging materials.

I am now Buyer - Packaging Materials for the Wharton Paper Company, a $1.6 billion manufacturer of consumer paper products and sanitary tissues. As such, I purchase over $30 million of packaging materials and vital supplies annually. This includes polywrap, folding cartons, and corrugated containers for the company's four manufacturing plants.

Enclosed is a current resume for your records. Although salary is not my first consideration, minimum compensation requirements are in the $85,000 plus range.

Should my qualifications be a match for one of your search assignments, I would appreciate hearing from you. Thank you for your consideration.

Sincerely yours,

Eugene A. Dromeshauser

Eugene A. Dromeshauser

EAD/mmb

Enclosure

36 Winchip Road
Princeton, NJ 08979

August 12, 2003

Ms. Dana Willis
The Corporate Source Group
1 Cranberry Hill
Lexington, MA 021743

Dear Ms. Willis:

I am an accomplished sales professional with four years' experience selling complex business systems to a variety of business applications. The enclosed resume details the specifics of my experience and accomplishments, however, I would like to highlight the fact that I have been the Top Regional Sales Representative for the Eastern Region for the last three years running.

I am seeking a senior sales or district sales management position selling "big ticket" business systems (i.e., computers, mailing systems, microfilm systems) to governmental agencies, manufacturing and/or services businesses. I especially enjoy selling complex systems that require applications problem solving for marketing success. This is an area of particular strength for me, and one which I find very satisfying.

Briefly, my qualifications include a B.S. degree in Psychology from the University of Maryland and four years selling microfilm systems for the Berry Corporation. During this period, I increased territory sales by 150% and have replaced competition at several leading accounts. Major customers include: U.S. Department of Labor, U.S. Department of the Navy, DuPont, IBM, General Dynamics, and Black & Decker, to mention a few.

If any of your client companies are looking for an accomplished sales professional with strong background in business systems sales, I would welcome the opportunity to talk with them. Compensation requirements are in the $95,000 range, and I am open to relocation to most areas of the country. I am also willing to travel extensively.

Thank you for your review of my qualifications, and I hope to hear from you shortly.

Sincerely,

Christopher T. Beatty

Christopher T. Beatty

Enclosure

JEFFREY A. MORSE
3601 Algonquin Road
Birmingham, AL 48009

March 15, 2004

The Walker Group, Inc.
2600 Fernbrook Lane, Suite 106
Minneapolis, MN 55447

Dear Sir/Madam:

This summer I will be completing my obligation as an officer in the United States Navy and will be making the transition to civilian employment. A complete resume detailing my qualifications is enclosed for your reference.

The following highlights my job search objectives:

EMPLOYMENT OBJECTIVE:	Engineering or engineering project management
PREFERRED LOCATION:	Greater Philadelphia area (open to other geographical locations)
SALARY REQUIREMENTS:	Flexible -- $60,000 minimum
AVAILABILITY:	Late July, 2004

If you are aware of any positions with your client companies that would allow me to utilize and refine my engineering and/or engineering management skills, please call. I look forward to hearing from you.

Thank you.

Sincerely,

Jeffrey A. Morse

Jeffrey A. Morse

Enclosure

GEORGE G. ATKINSON

719 Lighthouse Road
Hilton Head, SC 19928

Home: (913) 747-3127
Office: (913) 631-2077

June 1, 2003

Mr. H. G. Sloane
Sloane, Sloane & Smith
4405 Steubenville Pike
Pittsburgh, PA 15205

Dear Mr. Sloane:

I am writing to inquire about possible positions with any of your clients as a General Manager or Plant Manager in the chemical and related industries.

As Plant Manager for a large chemical company, I brought the operation from a $12 million loss to a $7 million profit in only seven years. I used TQM methods to achieve significant cost reductions and productivity improvements, via personnel training and development. Strong client orientation and business team interaction are competencies that created solid market penetration through an improved level of service and customer-focused product enhancements.

As the enclosed resume shows, I have over 15 years of extensive, diversified experience in the chemical industry. I would like to bring my track record for cost reduction and product development to an entrepreneurial, growing organization that can benefit from my extensive knowledge and experience.

As a follow up to this correspondence, I will plan to call to determine what, if any, opportunities may exist with your clients. If no appropriate opportunities exist, I would welcome your ideas and counsel concerning my current job search.

Thank you for your time, and I look forward to talking with you shortly.

Sincerely,

George G. Atkinson

George G. Atkinson

GGA:bas

Enclosure

KARLA B. REDDINGTON

519 Redwood Lane, Indianapolis, Indiana 66211   *(603) 927-8147*

June 20, 2004

Mr. Sean T. Radster
M. Shirley & Associates, Inc.
2030 Fairburn Avenue, Ste. 100
Los Angeles, CA 90025

Dear Mr. Radster:

I am a graduate of the University of Pennsylvania's Wharton School with an MBA in Finance and three years experience as a Financial Analyst with the Drummond Aerospace Corporation here in Indianapolis. I have decided to make a career change and am interested in finding a similar position with a company in the consumer products industry. Perhaps one of your clients may have an interest in my background.

The following have been some key accomplishments at Drummond:

- Developed manufacturing cost projections and funding requirements for a $200 million missile guidance project

- Secured funding for $500 million business expansion at highly favorable terms

- Developed computer model for projection of manufacturing costs for new electronic subassemblies

- Recipient of two government commendations for outstanding achievement in financial planning

I am motivated and ambitious, and am targeting only those companies offering clearly defined professional growth opportunities earned through knowledge and contribution to the business. Realistic opportunities for short-term advancement into management will also be an important factor in my decision.

I prefer the Midwest, with a particular interest in the Chicago area. However, I am open to other locations. Compensation requirements are in the $90,000 range.

I look forward to hearing from you shortly, should you have an appropriate opportunity that you feel may be of interest to me. Thank you for your consideration.

Sincerely,

Karla B. Reddington

Karla B. Reddington

Enclosure

DAVID R. SWANSON
40 Boulder Avenue
Charlestown, RI 02813

February 18, 2003

The Lowell Agency
12200 Park Central Drive
Suite 120
Dallas, TX 75251

Dear Sir/Madam:

I am an experienced Accounting executive seeking an opportunity for further career advancement in accounting/financial management. An overview of my experience and accomplishments are provided in the enclosed resume.

My ability to creatively deal with rapid growth and to manage and develop people, in addition to my professional qualifications, are well documented and should allow me to make a significant contribution to the right company.

I have no geographical restrictions, and salary requirements are negotiable as appropriate to the nature of the opportunity and geographic location.

Since my current employer is unaware of my decision to leave, I would appreciate your treating this inquiry with appropriate sensitivity.

I can be reached discreetly at work, (217) 362-9171 or through my wife at home, (217) 848-4397.

Thank you for your consideration.

Sincerely,

David R. Swanson

David R. Swanson

DRS:jls

Enclosure

WILLIAM T. FAULKNER
136 Oak Knoll
Mountain Lakes, NJ 07046

July 11, 2004

Ms. Beverly Kiplinger
B. Kiplinger & Associates
1107 Kenilworth Drive, Ste. 208
Baltimore, MD 21204

Dear Ms. Kiplinger:

Enclosed please find my resume.

I possess a record of significant accomplishment in senior-level Marketing/Sales Management positions along with early exposure to Accounting and Finance. My experience has been gained in diverse situations ranging from new ventures and business development/acquisitions, to two highly successful turnarounds.

My objective is to continue progression in the Marketing/Sales Management field or to pursue an opportunity in General Management. I would appreciate being considered for any opportunity you deem appropriate.

Thank you in advance for your consideration. I look forward to speaking with you in the near future.

Sincerely,

William T. Faulkner

William T. Faulkner

WTF:cab

Enclosure

KEITH W. BRAXTON
819 Devonshire Road
New Rochelle, NY 10804

July 16, 2005

Mr. Michael S. Silvon
Silvon & Associates
Executive Search Consultants
9 Wakefield Road, Suite 200
Lake Bluff, IL 60044

Dear Mr. Silvon:

It has come to my attention that your firm specializes in executive search consulting in the Human Resources field. Since I am a specialist seeking a senior-level Staffing position, it seems appropriate to forward my resume for your review.

As my resume shows, I hold an M.S. in Psychology from the University of Michigan and have over 14 years experience in Human Resources with nearly 10 years in Staffing. I am currently Director of Staffing Services for Beecham Laboratories, a $1.5 billion manufacturer of proprietary pharmaceuticals. In this capacity, I manage a staff of five professionals and provide corporate-wide recruiting and internal staffing support to a five-plant, 22,000 employee organization.

My wife, Peggy, has just completed her Master's degree at Columbia's School of Engineering & Applied Science and has received an excellent employment offer from Ford Aerospace in Orlando. We both enjoy sailing and have always been attracted to the Florida area. This offers the perfect opportunity for us to make a move.

Please consider my credentials for any employment-related search assignments you are currently conducting for firms located in the Orlando or surrounding areas (up to 1-1/2 hours commute). Although I would prefer an assignment at the Director level, I realize that I may need to be flexible in order to realize my geographical objective. Minimum compensation requirements are in the mid $80,000 range.

Thank you for taking the time to review my credentials, and I look forward to hearing from you.

Sincerely,

Keith W. Braxton

Keith W. Braxton

Enclosure

BRENDA A. RESTON
766 West Rolling Road
State College, PA 15332

January 3, 2003

Ms. Violet Bradley
The Bradley Agency
40 Cutter Mill Road
Great Neck, NY 11021

Dear Ms. Bradley:

I will be receiving an MBA in Finance from the Smeal School of Business in June of this year, and I am seeking a position as a Financial Analyst with a high-technology manufacturing or research company in Florida or one of the Southern Coastal States. My husband, Warren, and I are avid sailors and our objective is to be near a large body of water.

Besides graduating with honors in Finance, highlights of my qualifications include two years of employment as a Contract Cost Accountant with Belvar Electronics, Inc. and two summers of employment in the Corporate Finance Department of Lockheed Martin's Aerospace Division in Valley Forge, PA. While at Lockheed Martin, I handled financial projections for several classified electronics projects.

Compensation requirements are in the high $80,000 range. Should you be aware of a suitable opportunity with one of your clients, I would appreciate hearing from you.

Thank you for your consideration.

Very truly yours,

Brenda A. Reston

Brenda A. Reston

Enclosure

AGNES M. RUFENACH

310 Normandy Road
Bryn Mawr, PA 19110

Home: (610) 739-7052
Office: (610) 471-2412

May 16, 1996

Mr. Richard J. Morgan
Morgan Samuels Co., Inc.
6 Bemiston Avenue, Ste. 1212
St. Louis, MO 63105

Dear Mr. Morgan:

I am an experienced Architectural Engineer with over ten years experience in architectural design of commercial high-rise structures. Most recently, I was the Lead Engineer in the design of Liberty Place, the 62-story commercial high-rise building that now dominates the Philadelphia skyline and has won numerous national design awards.

Other major projects with which I have played a key design role include the Baltimore Aquarium, Skyline Towers (a 32-story office building in Baltimore), and Surrey Place West (a 22-story office complex in Washington, D.C.). In my 10-1/2 years in the Architectural Design field, I have won over 20 national and local awards for design excellence.

Unfortunately, Philmore Associates, Inc., the major development firm with which I have been associated since the beginning of my career, has just filed for Chapter Eleven bankruptcy and a massive reorganization of the company is now underway. It seems appropriate at this time for me to think about moving on with my career.

I am seeking a senior engineering or management position with a major developer or architectural engineering firm specializing in the design and/or construction of commercial high-rise structures. Compensation requirements are in the six figure range, and I would prefer an equity position in the firm, if available.

Relocation is no obstacle. I am quite willing to go where the opportunity is, however, I do have a preference for the Northeast. Overseas assignments will also be considered.

Should one of your clients have an appropriate position which you feel may be of interest to me, I would appreciate a call. Thank you for your consideration.

Sincerely,

Agnes M. Rufenach

Agnes M. Rufenach

Enclosure

1926 Peele Street
Sacramento, CA 94903

April 15, 2004

Mr. Wendel P. Manchester
Manchester & Associates
One Northgate Drive, 2nd Floor
San Francisco, CA 94111

Dear Mr. Manchester:

I was informed by a colleague that your firm specializes in the placement of Materials and Logistics professionals. I am thus enclosing my resume for your consideration.

As my resume shows, I have a B.S. in Business Administration from Lafayette College and three years experience in Procurement with Sanford Pharmaceuticals here in Sacramento. Some key accomplishments follow:

- Saved $1.3 million through negotiation of two-year contract on knock-down cartons at a price 20% below past pricing level

- Used computer analysis to adjust order cycle on polywrap, reducing inventory by 36% ($3/4 million savings annually)

- Modified and installed raw material computer system allowing greater control and accuracy in forecasting and planning raw materials and supplies inventory requirements

Sanford Pharmaceuticals, as you may be aware, was recently acquired by Fenwick Corporation, a London-based pharmaceutical giant. Fenwick has announced plans to cut back on the management staff at Sanford. This does not appear to bode well for immediate career growth. Since I am early in my career and career growth is important to me, I have elected to seek opportunities elsewhere.

Should one of your clients be looking for a motivated, ambitious Procurement professional with a strong work ethic and a demonstrated drive for bringing continuous improvement to business systems and processes, I hope that you will contact me.

Thank you for reviewing my credentials, and I hope to hear from you in the near future.

Sincerely,

Hall R. Peyton

Hall R. Peyton

Enclosure

SHARON D. BRUSTER
870 Hunt Club Lane
Danville, PA 15791

March 25, 2003

The Johnson Group, Inc.
1 World Trade Center, Suite 2020
New York, NY 10048-0202

Dear Sir/Madam:

I am an honors engineering student at Bucknell University and will be graduating with a B.S. in Mechanical Engineering in May of this year.

I am in search of an entry-level position as a Project Engineer in the central engineering department of a manufacturing company. I would enjoy being involved with the engineering, installation and start-up of manufacturing equipment as well as general plant facilities engineering work.

Besides my academic achievement, I have been active in athletics and have been a member of the Varsity Crew Team for the last three years. I have a balanced perspective and maintain involvement in a wide range of diverse activities.

Last summer I was an Engineering Intern with The Clorox Company, where I worked in their central engineering department as a Design Engineer in support of plant capital projects. Although I enjoyed working at Clorox, unfortunately there is a hiring freeze that will not allow the opportunity for employment at this time.

Should one of your client companies have room in their organization for a bright, eager, young Project Engineer, I would appreciate a call. Thank you for your time and consideration.

Sincerely,

Sharon D. Bruster

Sharon D. Bruster

Enclosure

RONALD L. GEORGE
1633 Gypsy Lane
Germantown, PA 19444

September 16, 2002

Ms. Constance A. Springer
Catalyx Group, Inc.
20 N. Wacker Drive, Suite. 3119
Chicago, IL 60606-3101

Dear Ms. Springer:

My company has recently been sold, and the new owners have chosen to manage the business themselves. I am therefore looking for a new opportunity in a senior operating role such as President and CEO, COO, or Vice President and General Manager.

While I would prefer to remain in the medical/surgical products or consumer health and beauty aids industries, where I have been particularly successful, I would also consider appropriate opportunities with companies outside these fields. Additionally, I would give serious consideration to new business start-up opportunities offering a "sweat equity" position in senior management.

If you currently have a search assignment that fits these requirements, I would be pleased to hear from you.

My compensation requirements are in the low six figure range, and I am open to relocation for a suitable opportunity.

Thank you for your consideration.

Sincerely,

Ronald L. George

Ronald L. George

RLG/tad

Enclosure

ALICE B. CHEN

---

801 Forsyth Boulevard, Clayton, MO 63105   **Phone: (917) 432-1284**

August 21, 2004

Mr. Anthony J. Myers
Carlyle Associates
33 Main Street
Stamford, CT 06901

Dear Mr. Myers:

Atlas Paper Company has recently announced a 25% cutback in its Technology Department. Unfortunately, as one of the least senior employees, I will be affected.

I hold a B.S. degree in Electrical Engineering from the University of Missouri and have two years experience as a Development Engineer with the Control System Development Group at Atlas. In this capacity, I work with the Process Development Group in the first-time application of computer control systems to novel, state-of-the-art papermaking and converting processes. The following are some of my accomplishments:

- Engineered entire process control system for prototype nonwoven materials manufacturing process

- Assisted Central Engineering with the first line scale-up of new diaper converting process, with responsibility for leading scale-up of distributed control systems

- Engineered motor control system for new pilot-scale paper machine

I have a strong background in the design, engineering, installation and start-up of a wide range of instrumentation and control systems. Additionally, I have the ability to apply this knowledge to both pilot and full-scale manufacturing equipment. I am also equally at home with both chemical and mechanical process applications.

My resume is enclosed for your review. I am seeking a Control Systems Engineering position in either a plant manufacturing or research laboratory setting and would welcome the opportunity to talk with any of your client companies for whom my background and interests are an appropriate fit.

Compensation requirements are in the $70,000 to $75,000 range, and I am open to opportunities with any of your clients located in the Midwest. Thank you for your consideration.

Sincerely,

Alice B. Chen

Alice B. Chen

Enclosure

CARTER D. JACKSON

818 Kimberly Lane, Malvern, PA 33607   Phone: (610)407-3572   Email: Carter818@AOL.com

April 19, 2004

Ms. Judith Blumenthal
Blumenthal Partners
393 Main Street
Raleigh, NC 27615

Dear Ms. Blumenthal:

Enclosed please find my resume, detailing a short but highly successful career in sales and marketing.

Currently, I am a Sales Representative in eastern Pennsylvania for Clarion Metals, a $100 million manufacturer of metal fasteners sold to the hardware trade in the Northeastern United States.

During my first two years selling for Clarion, I have more than doubled my territory sales volume, from $10 million to over $22 million. The company is obviously pleased with my performance!

Unfortunately, Clarion is a family-owned company and long-range career development opportunities appear rather limited. As I look at the senior-level positions within the company (i.e., Director and above), it is painfully obvious that being a member of the Clarion family is an absolute prerequisite. It is clear, if I am to grow professionally and financially, therefore, I must move on with my career.

Please review the enclosed resume against your current search assignments for sales and marketing professionals. I have an excellent track record and will prove a strong producer for any of clients who can use my background and experience.

Compensation requirements are in the $70,000 range, and I am receptive to relocation in the Southeastern United States. Thank you for your consideration.

Sincerely,

Carter D. Jackson

Carter D. Jackson

Enclosure

NICHOLAS B. EVANS
404 Plymouth Circle
Cincinnati, OH 45409

March 29, 2005

Mr. Roger S. Claxton
The Claxton Company
434 Greentree Center
Atlanta, GA 30328

Dear Mr. Claxton:

With today's economic environment and continued pressure on debt, cash flow, and profitability, companies need people who can make a difference. I can help!

My credentials are strong in Finance, Treasury, and Business Development/Planning. My track record demonstrates solid financial, business, and leadership competencies. For example:

- After being asked to corral a renegade marketing group, I added numerous controls and won the confidence of marketing as a business partner. The result – sales increases of over 25% and 50% in profits. Today, we are taking ownership of additional product lines with an annual target of $290 million in sales.

- After a merger, I was asked to redesign the cash management network and U.S. order review process. The result -- $37 million annual savings, tighter controls, and greater customer satisfaction.

- Worked closely with investment bankers to develop innovative financing and investment programs. The result -- savings of $1.3 million per year.

I now seek a new, more challenging career option. I can produce similar results elsewhere, perhaps for one of your clients needing someone like me.

If I am a fit for one of your current search assignments, I would welcome the opportunity to meet with you. Thank you for your consideration.

Sincerely,

Nicholas B. Evans

Nicholas B. Evans

Enclosure

KIMBERLY E. WAKEFIELD

541 Cumberland Avenue, Houston, TX 77042 / Phone: (714)397-4125 / Email: Kimwake@MSN.com

October 15, 2003

Mr. Thomas McCarthy
Empire Executive Search
1147 Lancaster Avenue
Berwyn, PA 19312

Dear Mr. McCarthy:

Enclosed is my updated resume that outlines my 15+ years experience in IS.

The focus of my career has been on the development, implementation and integration of management information systems in four major industries: Health Care, Government, Retail, and Manufacturing.

I can provide numerous references from both my current employer, as well as current and past clients, regarding my achievements and contributions.

Please contact me at my office (714) 644-3039 or home (714) 397-4125 with any questions you may have concerning my qualifications.

Thank you for your consideration, and I look forward to hearing from you regarding appropriate opportunities that may exist with your clients.

Sincerely,

Kimberly E. Wakefield

Kimberly E. Wakefield

Enclosure

GLORIA A. STEPHENSON

101 Bayhill Drive
Jacksonville, FL 32202   Email: GSteph@AOL.com   Home: (904) 928-1736
                                                               Office: (904) 279-3000

May 12, 2003

Mr. James A. Hayden
Hayden Group, Inc.
10 High Street
Boston, MA 02110

Dear Mr. Hayden:

During the past eight years I have played a major role in revitalizing the chemicals and specialties businesses of the Worthington Corporation in New York City.

Following an initial assignment as Director of Sales for the Chemicals Division, I was promoted to division General Manager, taking P&L responsibility for several key businesses including three foreign subsidiaries.

My team's efforts contributed to the major growth in sales, profit contribution, and return on investment of the division, recently renamed the Specialty Products Division.

As a result of the recent sale of this division, I have elected to make a career change and am writing to ask your help. A resume, which details my accomplishments at Worthington Corporation as well as my eight years at Dow Chemical, is attached.

Compensation and location are secondary to opportunity. Ideally, I'd like an assignment at either the general management or senior corporate marketing/sales management level, with an opportunity to match or better my 2002 total cash compensation of $156,000.

If my background should match any of your current or near future search assignments, I would be pleased to meet with you at your convenience. Thank you for your consideration.

Sincerely,

Gloria A. Stephenson

Gloria A. Stephenson

Enclosure

WILBER S. LLOYD
Smyrna, DE 19898
722 Hummingbird Lane

July 16, 2004

Ms. Carol G. Newman
Newman & Newman Co., Ltd.
48 Helen Drive
Queensbury, NY 12804

Dear Ms. Newman:

If one of your client companies is in search of a seasoned, results-oriented sales executive to lead their sales and marketing function, you may want to give careful consideration to my qualifications.

Review of the enclosed resume will reveal I have over 15 years of sales management experience, with demonstrated leadership ability in motivating sales organizations to consistently achieve record sales performance. In my last three positions, for example, the groups I managed set new sales records each and every year, with an average annual increase of nearly 20%!

My qualifications include an M.B.A. in Marketing from the University of Connecticut and nearly 18 years in consumer product sales. For the last four years I have been Regional Sales Manager for Lever Brother's Northeast Region, where I manage an 80-person sales organization covering a ten-state area.

My current compensation is $155,000, consisting of a base salary of $120,000 and bonus of $35,000. I am seeking a position at the national sales or sales/marketing level with broader accountability and the opportunity for substantial earnings improvement.

I would be pleased to meet with you to further discuss my credentials and to explore appropriate management opportunities with your clients. Thank you for your consideration, and I look forward to hearing from you.

Sincerely,

Wilber S. Lloyd

Wilber S. Lloyd

Enclosure

SANDRA R. BERMUDEZ

255 Cedar Valley Drive
Highland Park, IL 60035   Email: SRB255@AOL.com   Home: (312) 633-7147
                                                           Office: (312) 593-9098

August 22, 2002

Mr. Robert M. Montgomery
R.M. Montgomery Assoc., Inc.
55 Madison Ave., Ste. 200
Morristown, NJ 07960

Dear Mr. Montgomery:

My research indicates your firm specializes in executive search consulting in the financial field. Since I am searching for a position in financial management, I have therefore enclosed my resume for review against your clients' current needs.

Briefly, my credentials include an M.B.A. in Finance from the University of Vermont and ten years' experience in finance with Barrington Industries, where I am now Manager of Corporate Finance. Barrington Industries, as you may know, is a $500 million manufacturer of floor coverings. In this capacity, I manage a six-person department with functional responsibility for domestic and international finance, money & banking, financial planning & analysis, and treasury.

It appears my career has peaked here at Barrington, since the Chief Financial Officer is only two years my senior and is planning to remain with the company. I am therefore seeking a position as Chief Financial Officer with a small to medium-sized manufacturing company, where I can report to the Chief Executive Officer and assume total responsibility for the firm's financial function.

My compensation requirements are in the $100,000 to $115,000 range.

Thank you for reviewing my credentials. I look forward to hearing from you should you feel I would be a suitable match for one of your current or future search assignments.

Very truly yours,

Sandra R. Bermudez

Sandra R. Bermudez

Enclosure

MAURICE ESTUARDO CHAVEZ
101 W. Eagle Road
Havertown, PA 19083
(215) 499-8032

July 15, 2004

Mr. Peter R. Hendelman
PRH Management, Inc.
2777 Summer Street
Stamford, CT 06905

Dear Mr. Hendelman:

I am advised by one of my colleagues that your firm has some specialization in conducting search assignments in the field of distribution management. I am pleased, therefore, to forward a copy of my resume for review against your current search projects.

My qualifications include a B.A. in Business Administration from Villanova University and 18 years' distribution management, most of which has been with Burlington Industries, where I am currently Corporate Manager of Warehousing and Distribution. In this capacity, I report to the Vice President of Logistics and manage a 350-employee, 12-warehouse transportation and distribution function for this $6 billion corporation.

During the last three years, under my leadership, Burlington has realized over $25 million in annual cost savings as I streamlined distribution operations and implemented far-reaching strategies aimed at productivity improvement. I am currently directing four major new initiatives that should add another $8 to $10 million annual cost savings to the bottom line over the next two years.

Perhaps one of your clients might be interested in my credentials and ability to bring similar cost savings and efficiencies to their operations. If so, I would welcome the opportunity to meet with you to explore this possibility.

I am seeking a position at the Director level in distribution management with full accountability for a company's distribution planning and operations. Compensation requirements are in the $95,000 to $100,000 range, dependent upon location and nature of the position.

Thank you for your consideration and I look forward to hearing from you should you have an appropriate opportunity to discuss with me.

Sincerely,

Maurice Estuardo Chavez

Maurice Estuardo Chavez

Enclosure

REGINALD T. HARRISON
1722 Whitehall Avenue
Brockton, MA 02401

September 2, 2004

Mr. R. J. Wymar
Wytmar & Co., Inc.
254 Donlea Road
Barrington, IL 60010

Dear Mr. Wymar:

I understand that your company enjoys an excellent reputation as a retained executive search firm in the marketing field. Perhaps you may have an active search assignment for a senior marketing executive with my credentials.

My qualifications include an M.B.A. in Marketing from the University of Michigan and some 16 years' marketing and sales experience in the specialty chemicals field. Currently Director of Marketing for the Specialty Chemicals Division of Dow Chemical Company, I manage a staff of 12 brand managers, market analysts and research support personnel in the marketing of a wide range of specialty chemicals sold to numerous industrial applications.

During my last three years in this position, we have successfully introduced over 15 products, accounting for over $400 million in new sales. All but one product entry has either reached or exceeded sales expectations, with better than half the products surpassing first-year goals by more than 25%.

I am now seeking a position as either vice president or director of marketing/sales at the corporate level. Obviously, my strength is in the chemical or specialty chemicals field. Compensation requirements are in the $140+ range, and I will consider relocation to most areas of the country.

Should you have an appropriate search assignment that is a match for my qualifications and interests, I would welcome a call. Thank you for your consideration.

Sincerely,

Reginald T. Harrison

Reginald T. Harrison

Enclosure

WILMA B. HARRIS
23 Orchard Road
Elsmere, DE 19384

January 16, 2003

Mr. Blake D. Edwards
The Edwards Group
909 Blue Grass Plaza, SW
Lexington, KY 57027

Dear Mr. Edwards:

As an employment agency specializing in the recruitment of engineering talent for the pulp and paper industry, you may have some interest in my background. A resume is enclosed for your reference.

Briefly, I am a mechanical engineer with strong project background in the converting of coated and fine papers. I hold a B.S. degree from the University of Maryland and have spent the last five years as a project engineer with the Carver Paper Company at their Hastings Mill. As you are likely aware, this mill is currently for sale and future career opportunities are therefore uncertain.

I am seeking a position as a senior project engineer or engineering manager within the paper industry, with a particular interest in either papermaking or converting. Assignments in general mill engineering would not be of interest to me.

I am completely open to relocation, and my salary requirements are in the $75,000 to $80,000 range.

Since my employer is unaware of my decision to make a change, I ask that my candidacy be handled with appropriate discretion.

Thank you for your assistance . I look forward to hearing from you should you identify a suitable opportunity that you feel may be of interest to me.

Sincerely,

Wilma B. Harris

Wilma B. Harris

Enclosure

ROGER P. PERSHING
6 Willingham Court
Augusta, GA 30836

March 23, 2003

Mr. Marshall W. Rotella, Jr.
The Corporate Connection
7024 Glen Forest Drive
Richmond, VA 23226

Dear Mr. Rotella:

I have recently learned of your firm's specialization in executive search consulting in the field of operations management. Enclosed, therefore, please find a copy of my resume for review against current or future search assignments.

My qualifications include a B.S. in Mechanical Engineering from Georgia Tech, followed by an M.B.A. from M.I.T.'s Sloan School of Business. Since graduation from Sloan in 1996, I have been in manufacturing management with General Electric Company's Small Motors' Division.

In the last seven years since joining G.E., I have experienced rapid advancement, starting with a position as Manufacturing Supervisor at a small motors manufacturing facility in Rochester, New York, and culminating with my current assignment as General Manager for a 1,200-employee manufacturing facility located in Batesburg, South Carolina. Details of my various assignments and specific accomplishments are highlighted on the enclosed resume.

I am seeking a senior-level manufacturing position at the director or vice president level, with full P&L responsibility for a multi-plant operation. My preference would be to remain within the electrical field, since I already have seven years invested in this industry. Compensation requirements are in the $125,000 base range plus bonus.

Should one of your clients be looking for a fast-track manufacturing executive with excellent experience and solid accomplishments in the electrical field, I would appreciate hearing from you.

Thank you for your consideration.

Sincerely,

Roger P. Pershing

Roger P. Pershing

Enclosure

4

Advertising Response Cover Letters

Employment advertising has historically been a major source of jobs for those engaged in a job-hunting campaign. Today, this includes those positions also advertised on the Internet which is, in fact, rapidly replacing the far more expensive advertising found in newspaper want ads. Although specific estimates vary, studies show that print advertising, whether newspaper, professional/trade journal, or Internet, accounts for an estimated 10 to 14% of all jobs that are found.

Knowing how to effectively respond to recruitment advertising is, therefore, an important element of your job hunting effort. How effectively you respond to such advertising has a definite bearing on whether an employment interview will follow. Poorly written letters that contain improper grammar, typos, or lack adequate focus can lead to ruined employment chances. By contrast, well-written cover letters can often help land that all-important employment interview.

THE ADVERTISING ADVANTAGE

The key advantage of the advertising cover letter, when compared to other cover letters the job seeker must write, is that the author knows precisely what the employer is seeking. In far too many cases, however, this fact is clearly lost on the job seeker, and so is the opportunity to make the sale!

As an experienced employment professional, I am often amazed how many job seekers ignore an employer's specifics as stated in the ad and go on to describe qualifications in no way related to the employer's needs. What a shame to miss such a golden opportunity!

This behavior is reminiscent of the salesperson who doesn't take the time to "qualify" the buyer. In such cases, the sales representative fails to query the buyer sufficiently at the beginning of the sales presentation to understand what factors are *key motivators* that will cause the buyer to buy the product. The salesperson drones on and on about the product's many features, but is clueless about those features most important to the buying decision. The result is "no sale!"

The successful sales representative, by contrast, first determines what product attributes are most important to the buyer's purchasing decision. By focusing the sales presentation on these motivating factors, the representative substantially increases probability of a sale.

BEN FRANKLIN BALANCE SHEET

A good technique to use when preparing to write an advertising response cover letter is the *Ben Franklin Balance Sheet.* This approach is used to qualify the buyer (the employer) and to force yourself to focus only on those candidate qualifications that are important to the employer's hiring decision.

To use this approach, draw a line down the center of a blank piece of paper. Label the left column "Employer's Requirements." Title the right column "My Qualifications."

Now, carefully review the employment advertisement line by line, and list each of the employer's specific requirements on the left side of your balance sheet. Prioritize these key requirements on the basis of the emphasis the employer appears to place on each in the ad. Key terms such as "must have," "prefer," "highly desirable," provide strong clues about the importance the employer attaches to certain candidate qualifications. Also, the order in which these qualifications appear in the advertisement frequently indicates their relative importance. Often the most critical qualifications are listed first, with the least important listed last.

Now, using your resume, prepare a corresponding list of those qualifications you possess that coincide with the employer's requirements. Record them on the right side of your balance sheet under the heading "My Qualifications" and adjacent to the relevant Employer's Requirements.

This simple analysis will help you write a very effective cover letter specifically tailored to the needs of the employer. The basic data are readily available and are organized in the order of greatest importance to the employer. You are now ready to "make the sale."

LETTER COMPONENTS

The sample advertising response letters found in this chapter contain certain key elements, including:

1. Reference to advertisement.
2. Expression of interest in position.
3. Comparison of employer's requirements with personal qualifications.
4. Salary requirements statement (optional).
5. Request for response or interview.
6. Statement of appreciation.

The sample letters illustrate the different ways these elements can be effectively incorporated into an advertising response letter.

TWO FORMATS

The advertising response cover letter normally uses one of two formats: The *linear* format or the *literary* format. Review of the sample resumes provided in this chapter shows several approaches to the use of each.

The linear approach is generally used when the author wants to highlight that he or she has *all* of the employer's key requirements. The writer provides a line-by-line (linear) listing of these qualifications. This approach highlights these qualifications and facilitates the employer's direct comparison with its own requirements. This format aligns directly with the stated candidate requirements contained in the employment ad and, if well presented, should systematically lead the employer to conclude that you are well-qualified for the position and that an employment interview is clearly in order.

The literary (paragraph) format, on the other hand, is most frequently used when the author does not possess all of the key qualifications stated in the advertisement. In such cases, the linear approach should be avoided, and the writer should instead use the literary format.

As with the linear format, a parallel should be drawn between your qualifications and the employer's requirements. The literary approach, however, makes it far less obvious to the employer that certain key qualifications are missing. By contrast, the linear approach would highlight these voids, often causing the employer to eliminate you from further hiring consideration.

The Ben Franklin Balance Sheet will serve you well when choosing which format to use. Use of the balance sheet will make it clear which of the employer's qualifications you are missing and should make it fairly easy for you to choose the letter format that will best serve your needs.

The balance of this chapter contains examples of employment advertisements along with their sample cover letter responses. You will note how effectively these letters employ the comparison techniques discussed in this chapter. Careful study of these sample letters should enable you to construct effective cover letters that significantly enhance the probabilities of landing employment interviews.

MANUFACTURING COST ACCOUNTANT

A $4.5 billion snack food manufacturer and industry leader, we have ten production facilities in the U.S. and extensive overseas operations. We are known for having an excellent reputation as an employer and are particularly noted for our commitment to employee development.

We are seeking a Manufacturing Cost Accountant for our 600-employee manufacturing facility in Wayne, NJ. This position reports to the Manager of Cost Accounting and has responsibility for all manufacturing accounting for eight product brands.

This position requires a B.A. degree in Accounting with at least one year of manufacturing cost accounting experience in a consumer or pharmaceutical products manufacturing operation. Must be thoroughly versed in standard accounting practices. Prefer CPA with prior Big 4 auditing background.

For immediate consideration, please send or e-mail resume with salary requirements to:

Attn: Human Resource Department

LITE-SNACKS, INC.
P.O. Box 1300
Austin , TX 19284

E-mail: HRD@LiteSnacks.com

Equal Opportunity Employer, M/F

LINDA E. GIBSON
1432 S. Wabash Street
Kokomo, IN 43621

June 24, 2004

Lite-Snacks, Inc.
ATTN: Human Resources Department
P.O. Box 1300
Austin, TX 19284

Dear Sir or Madam:

Your ad for a Manufacturing Cost Accountant in the June 12th issue of *The Fort Wayne Examiner* interests me, and I am therefore forwarding my resume for your review.

As my resume will attest, I have excellent qualifications for your opening. Please consider the following:

- B.A., Accounting, University of Cincinnati, 2001

- C.P.A., May 2003

- 1 year, Auditor, Coopers & Lybrand

- 1 year, Cost Accountant, Ross Laboratories, (Fort Wayne, IN, Plant)

- Well versed in standard cost accounting practices

My salary requirements are in the low $60,000 range.

Should you agree that my background is a good match for your requirements, I would welcome the opportunity to meet with you personally. I can be reached on a confidential basis during the day at (317) 992-3176.

Thank you for your consideration. I look forward to hearing from you.

Sincerely,

Linda E. Gibson

Linda E. Gibson

Enclosure

CORPORATE CONTROLLER

Floor Visions, Inc., is an $800 million manufacturer of quality hardwood flooring with distribution throughout the Northeastern United States. We are a 40-year-old company whose sales and profits have nearly tripled in the last 4 years alone.

The position of Corporate Controller reports to the Chief Financial Officer with responsibility for preparation of all quarterly and annual consolidated returns, S.E.C. reporting, accounts receivable, accounts payable, cost accounting, tax research and preparation, credit and audit. Reporting to this position are 6 managers and a staff of 16 professional and support personnel.

Successful candidates will possess a B.S. in Accounting and at least five years' corporate accounting management experience in a multi-plant, multi-state manufacturing environment. Must be thoroughly versed in preparation of consolidated statements, S.E.C. requirements and standard accounting practices. A CPA and at least two years' public accounting experience also required.

Highly competitive salary and attractive executive bonus program are provided. Comprehensive benefits program also furnished. For employment consideration, please forward or e-mail resume to:

ATTN: Gregory D. Banner

Floor Visions, Inc
24 East River Road
Atlanta, GA 48506-2114

E-mail: gbanner@FloorVisions.com

EOE

1402 Blythe Avenue
Drexel Hill, PA 19026

April 30, 2003

Mr. Gregory D. Banner
Floor Visions, Inc.
24 East River Road
Atlanta, GA 48506-2114

Dear Mr. Banner:

I am submitting my resume in response to your April 28th ad in the *Philadelphia Inquirer* for a Corporate Controller. This sounds like an interesting position, and I would welcome the opportunity to discuss it with you personally.

It would appear that my qualifications are an excellent match for your requirements.

In keeping with your specification, I hold a B.S. in Accounting from Widener University and have over five years' corporate accounting experience with Barter Brush Corporation, a manufacturer of paint brushes. Barter has six manufacturing facilities in five states.

As Manager of Corporate Accounting, I am responsible for preparation of the company's consolidated returns on both a quarterly and annual basis. I am well trained in standard accounting procedures and thoroughly versed in S.E.C. requirements.

I completed my C.P.A. in 1996 while an Auditor with Arthur Andersen. My credentials include over three years of public accounting experience.

I believe that I am well qualified for the position advertised, and I could make a meaningful contribution to your company. I hope we have the opportunity to meet to further discuss the specifics of your requirements.

Thank you for your consideration.

Sincerely,

Dawn M. Bedner

Dawn M. Bedner

DMB/rac

Enclosure

BRUCE W. NEWCOMB

302 Mountain Ridge Road		*Office: (518) 876-9314*
Utica, NY 14936	*FJT@MSN.com*	*Home: (518) 775-3047*

March 31, 2004

Mr. Thomas A. Harting
Employment Manager
PaperChem, Inc.
2388 Cole Street
Scranton, PA 17652

Dear Mr. Harting:

Your ad in the March 28th edition of the *Utica Daily News* for a Sales Representative - Specialty Chemicals caught my eye. This sounds like an exciting opportunity very much in keeping with my career objectives, and I would appreciate the chance to gain more insight into this position through personal discussion with you.

Careful review of your requirements suggests that I am well-qualified for this opportunity. Consider the following:

- B.S. degree in Chemical Engineering

- 3 years selling specialty chemicals to the corrugated industry

- General knowledge of papermaking processes

- Strong technical problem-solving skills (serve as regional resource on tough customer problems)

My interpersonal skills are solid, and I am frequently called upon to make important customer presentations due to my excellent communication and presentation skills. In addition, you might like to know that I was the leading Sales Representative in the Northeast Region in 2003.

Through review of my enclosed resume, I hope that you will conclude that I have the talent and motivation to make a strong contribution to PaperChem, and we will have the opportunity to personally meet in the near future.

Thank you for your consideration, and I look forward to hearing from you.

Very truly yours,

Bruce W. Newcomb

Bruce W. Newcomb

Enclosure

DIRECTOR
SALES & MARKETING

Auto Sealing Systems, a leading manufacturer of high-performance sealing systems and gasket products for automotive and industrial applications, is seeking a Director of Sales & Marketing to manage its corporate marketing and sales function.

Reporting to the President, this position will play a lead role in the development of the strategy needed to support the company's aggressive growth plans. Products are sold both direct and through distributor networks to O.E.M. accounts.

We seek a degreed executive with a strong background in marketing and sales management to O.E.M. accounts. Must be a talented leader/motivator with a solid track record of continuously achieving sales objectives. Requires good strategic thinker who can contribute to the management of the business as a member of the senior management team.

If qualified and interested in this position, please send or e-mail resume and salary history to:

Wilma G. Davidson
Executive Vice President

Auto Sealing Systems, Inc.
1842 West Goshen Avenue
Muncie, IN 47304-1332

E-mail: wilma_d@AutoSeal.com

Equal Opportunity Employer, M/F

DYLAN P. STENDLE

1200 Pea Patch Lane
Fort Wayne, IN 14203

DSten@MSN.com

Home: (716) 752-0337
Office: (716) 835-6800

October 16, 2003

Ms. Wilma G. Davidson
Executive Vice President
Auto Sealing Systems, Inc.
1842 West Goshen Avenue
Muncie, IN 47304-1332

Dear Ms. Davidson:

I am forwarding my resume in response to your October 15th ad in the *Indiana Star* for a Director - Sales & Marketing. This position sounds quite interesting, and I would appear to closely fit the candidate specifications as detailed in your ad.

Specifically, I hold an MBA in Marketing and have over ten years' marketing and sales management experience selling to O.E.M. accounts. As Director of Marketing for Fuel Jet Carburetors, I manage a 30-employee marketing and field sales organization selling automotive carburetors to car and truck engine manufacturers through both a distributor network and direct.

During the last five years, my marketing and sales strategies have led to a 250% increase in sales volume coupled with a profit increase of nearly 300%. I am known for being a key contributor to the business planning process and am credited with revitalizing and motivating the marketing and sales organization through creative leadership.

I would welcome the opportunity to meet with you to explore how I might bring added value to Auto Sealing Systems' marketing and sales effort through solid strategic planning and effective managerial leadership.

My current compensation is $150,000 ($100,000 base salary plus $50,000 bonus). I also have a company-furnished automobile and other minor executive perks.

Thank you for your consideration. I look forward to hearing from you.

Sincerely,

Dylan P. Stendle

Dylan P. Stendle

DPS:rms

FINANCIAL ANALYST

Fortune 100 consumer goods company seeks Financial Analyst for Corporate Planning Group.

Position reports to the Manager of Strategic Planning and will participate in the evaluation of various strategic business options including acquisitions & mergers, new business development, and expansion/consolidation of existing businesses. Will regularly interface with senior executive officers, including the presentation of study findings and recommendations regarding alternate business strategies.

Successful candidate will hold an MBA from a highly quantitative business school with emphasis in Finance. Must have excellent interpersonal and communications skills, including the presence and poise needed to interface effectively with executive level management. Some prior experience in merger and acquisition analysis highly desired.

Please forward or e-mail your resume and salary requirements to:

Ms. Margaret R. Temple
Corporate Employment Manager
(E-mail: MTemple@UHPI.com)

Universal Home Products, Inc.
815 Wacker Drive
Chicago, IL 19167-4850

Equal Opportunity Employer, M/F

Eileen A. Davis

747 Copperfield Avenue
Wilmington, DE 19898

Home: (302) 621-0973
Office: (302) 433-2076

February 22, 2002

Ms. Margaret R. Temple
Corporate Employment Manager
Universal Home Products, Inc.
815 Wacker Drive
Chicago, IL 19167-4850

Dear Ms. Temple:

I noted your ad for a Financial Analyst in this Sunday's edition of the *Delaware Star Ledger* with a great deal of interest. Your candidate description appears to be an excellent match with my personal profile.

Please consider the following:

- MBA, St. Joseph's University, Honors Graduate (Finance Major)

- Excellent communication skills:
  - Debate Team President, 2000 and 2001
  - Actress, four plays
  - English 101 (Freshman Composition), Grade = A

- Evidence of Interpersonal/Leadership Skills
  - Sorority President, two years
  - Sorority Vice President, one year

My extracurricular activities and summer work experience have enabled me to develop the poise and maturity needed to effectively relate to senior-level management. Additionally, I assisted in merger and acquisition analysis during my summer employment with the Sun Oil Company.

I believe that these qualifications, along with my drive and enthusiasm, make me an excellent candidate for your opening. I hope to have the opportunity to meet with you during a visit to Universal Home Products.

Thank you for your consideration.

Very truly yours,

Eileen A. Davis

Eileen A. Davis

Enclosure

VICE PRESIDENT
FINANCE

We are a $300 million manufacturer of electronic components for the defense industry. A large federal contract has necessitated that we triple our size in the next 10 months, requiring total restructuring of all financials.

Reporting directly to the Chief Financial Officer, this position has full responsibility for day-to-day direction of the company's financial functions including money & banking, domestic finance, international finance and credit.

We seek a seasoned financial manager with a minimum of 8 years' experience in the defense manufacturing industry. Must be thoroughly versed in financial theory and highly innovative in raising capital and restructuring corporate debt load.

Excellent interpersonal, communications and managerial skills also required.

Send or e-mail resume and compensation requirements to:

Box 1301
WASHINGTON POST
1150 15th Street, NW
Washington, DC 20071

E-mail: TofflerT146@AOL.com

Sydney R. Porter
816 Willow Street
Reston, VA 16273

August 14, 2003

Box 1301
Washington Post
1150 15th Street, NW
Washington, DC 20071

Dear Sir or Madam:

I am interested in talking with you concerning your need for a Vice President of Finance as described in your August 12th ad in the *Washington Post*. This appears to be an exciting opportunity, and I appear to have the profile that you seek.

My resume is enclosed for your review and consideration.

As specified in your advertisement, I am a seasoned financial manager with over eight years' experience in the defense manufacturing industry. Specifically, I am Manager of Corporate Finance with JetStar Electronics, a supplier of weaponry guidance systems for military vehicles.

My credentials include an MBA in Finance from the University of Chicago, and I am well-schooled in financial theory and its applications.

As evidence of my innovation, despite loss of its AA financial rating and an after-tax loss of $20 million in 2001, I was able to secure a $130 million line of credit at prime rate for JetStar. By restructuring the corporate debt load and providing the funding for a $100 million capital expansion program, JetStar was able to "turn the corner" and return to profitability.

Our 2002 after-tax profit was $22 million, a healthy 16% ROI! Additionally, our AA financial rating has been restored and JetStar is now on the "recommended buy" list of several of the nation's leading brokerage houses.

Perhaps I could make a similar contribution to your company. I would welcome the opportunity to explore this possibility during a personal interview.

I appreciate your consideration and look forward to hearing from you. Thank you.

Sincerely,

Sydney R. Porter

Sydney R. Porter

Enclosure

CYNTHIA D. DONNER

305 East 16th Street, Costa Mesa, CA 90334

May 22, 2003

Manager of Professional Employment
Harrington Cosmetics, Inc.
825 Watson Blvd.
Los Angeles, CA 12948-0117

Dear Sir/Madam:

You sparked my interest with your ad for a Marketing Brand Manager - Consumer Products in today's *Los Angeles Times*. This sounds like an exciting opportunity, and I would appear to have the qualifications you are seeking.

Please consider my credentials:

- MBA in Marketing, Stanford University, 1998

- 5 years' Consumer Marketing Experience (The Gillette Company, Corporate Marketing Department)

- Brand management marketing results include:

    - 20-point market share increase, *Foamy* shaving cream
    - 50% sales increase, *Chic* disposable razors
    - 14-point market share increase, *Buff-Away* exfoliating cleanser

I am noted for being an effective communicator and an excellent team player. I frequently serve as facilitator during business team meetings and am skilled at maximizing group participation and creating a feeling of "group ownership" around marketing plans and strategies. I am a strong advocate of the "participative" style of management and enjoy excellent interpersonal relationships with others.

Should you have an interest in me, I would be pleased to visit Harrington Cosmetics to further explore this opportunity with you and the members of your Marketing Staff.

Thank you for your consideration, and I look forward to hearing from you in the near future.

Sincerely,

Cynthia D. Donner

Cynthia D. Donner

Enclosure

ANDREW W. WELLSFIELD
12 Old Lake Road
Huron, OH 38495

November 5, 2003

Ms. Myra T. Williams
Vice President, Marketing
Microimage Systems, Inc.
500 Holyoke Road,
Springfield, MA 48596

Dear Ms. Williams:

Your November 4 ad in the *Cleveland Plain Dealer* for a Director of Marketing has stimulated considerable interest on my part. I am therefore submitting my resume for review and consideration.

Much of my background closely parallels your specific requirements, and I would appear to be well-qualified for this opportunity.

I hold an MBA in Marketing and am currently Manager of Marketing for ITA, a $300 million manufacturer of computer systems and software sold primarily to banks, insurance companies and government agencies. I am familiar with the financial record keeping requirements of these organizations.

Under my marketing leadership, ITA has more than doubled its annual sales in the last five years. This growth has been driven by the highly successful introduction of two new product lines -- ITA System IV and System V. Additionally, System I has been successfully repositioned in the market, resulting in a 15% gain in market share.

My knowledge of your target markets, coupled with demonstrated success in the marketing of major new system products, strongly suggests that I could make a significant contribution to your marketing and business objectives. Perhaps we could meet to more thoroughly explore this possibility.

My compensation requirements are in the low six-figure range.

I appreciate your consideration and look forward to the possibility of meeting with you and the members of your senior management team. Thank you.

Sincerely,

Andrew W. Wellsfield

Andrew W. Wellsfield

Enclosure

PROJECT ENGINEER

SkillCraft, Inc., the world's leader in the manufacture and sale of power tools, seeks Project Engineer for its 1,800-employee manufacturing facility in New Brooke, NY. This excellent opportunity will prove challenging for the fresh graduate looking for first exposure to a plant project engineering environment.

Reporting to a Senior Project Engineer, you will be responsible for assisting in the engineering, installation and start-up of small tool manufacturing equipment.

Our ideal candidate will have a B.S. in Mechanical Engineering and a strong desire for hands-on project work. Above-average academic performance and/or demonstrated leadership potential highly desirable.

Excellent compensation and out-standing benefits program provided.

Interested candidates should e-mail or send resume to:

Mr. William Davis
Technical Employment Manager
(E-mail: WDavis@SkillCraft.com)

SkillCraft, Inc.
25 Beacon Road
New Brooke, NY 89385

Equal Opportunity Employer

Colleen O. McRafter
23-A Warner Hall
Arizona State University
Phoenix, AZ 77845

April 2, 2003

Mr. William Davis
Technical Employment Manager
SkillCraft, Inc.
25 Beacon Road
New Brooke, NY 89385

Dear Mr. Davis:

The position of Project Engineer which you advertised in this Sunday's edition of the *Syracuse Gazette* sounds like the kind of job for which I am looking. Additionally, I would seem to be an excellent match for your requirements.

My qualifications include:

- B.S. in Mechanical Engineering, Arizona State University, May 2003

- Grade Point Average = 3.4/4.0

- Demonstrated leadership includes:
  - Captain, Varsity Swim Team, 2003
  - Vice President, KD Sorority, 2002
  - Vice President, A.S.M.E., 2002

I have always preferred hands-on as opposed to theoretical work. This is clearly demonstrated through several of my hobbies: auto repair/maintenance, furniture refinishing, construction and remodeling.

Additionally, my co-op assignment as Assistant Plant Project Engineer at Wheelright Corporation has provided me with practical, hands-on plant project engineering experience.

May I have the opportunity to meet with you and the members of your Plant Engineering Staff?

I look forward to hearing from you.

Sincerely,

Colleen O. McRafter

Colleen O. McRafter

Enclosure

DIRECTOR OF ENGINEERING

High-quality manufacturer of coated papers seeks executive to head its 45-employee corporate engineering group.

Position reports to Vice President – Corporate Engineering and is responsible, through engineering staff, for directing all capital project work, including mill construction, expansions and major rebuild projects. Will manage annual capital projects budget of $400 to $600 million.

Seek seasoned engineering manager with 15+ years' experience in the paper industry. Must demonstrate ability to effectively direct and manage sizeable engineering department with large scale, multiple project workload. Position requires enthusiastic advocate/practitioner of participative management who firmly believes in the importance of "employee stakeholders" as the key to high morale and increased productivity.

Highly competitive base salary plus executive bonus plan. Excellent range of cafeteria-style benefits also available.

For consideration, please forward or e-mail your complete resume and compensation requirements to:

Ms. Barbara A. Larson
Director of Employment
(Email: Babs@WindsorPaper.com)

Windsor Paper Company
Box 350
Racine, WI 75960

Equal Opportunity Employer

315 Green Meadow Drive
Marinette, WI 55467

February 2, 2003

Ms. Barbara A. Larson
Director of Employment
Windsor Paper Company
Box 350
Racine, WI 75960

Dear Ms. Larson:

I am forwarding my resume in response to your January 30th ad in the <u>Appleton Gazette</u> for the position of Director of Engineering. This appears to be an exciting opportunity and one for which I am well-qualified.

As called for in your advertisement, I am a seasoned engineering executive with over 15 years' experience in the paper industry. In my current position as Manager of Corporate Engineering for Appleton Paper Company, I direct a 40-employee central engineering group accountable for all capital project work (new equipment installation and rebuilds) at four papermaking and converting mills. Our annual capital budget is in the $300 to $500 million range.

Some major capital projects that I have directed include:

- Engineering & construction of Neenah, WI, Mill
  (40 TPD Corrugated Plant; Capital budget: $350 million)

- Complete rebuild of two fine paper machines
  (Madison, WI, Plant; Capital Expense: $210 million)

I am both a strong advocate and practitioner of the "participative" approach to management. I endeavor to involve my subordinates in all aspects of department operations, from strategic planning through day-to-day operations. I have personally led and facilitated several productivity task forces, which have included representation from all levels of the engineering organization. I recognize the value of the "employee stakeholder" concept.

I feel I have the qualifications to make a strong contribution to Windsor Paper's Central Engineering Group and hope that you agree. I would welcome the opportunity to meet with you. My compensation requirements are in the low $100K range.

I look forward to hearing from you shortly. Thank you.

Sincerely,

David R. Swanson

David R. Swanson

Enclosure.

ADMINISTRATIVE RECRUITER

We seek experienced recruiter to manage all administrative employment for our $500 million, multiplant baked goods manufacturing company.

Position reports to the Director of Human Resources and is responsible for the recruitment and hiring of all administrative, marketing and sales professionals.

Successful candidate will have a college degree coupled with 1-2 years' experience in a corporate employment environment. Should be knowledge-able concerning the cost effective use of employment sources, including college recruiting.

If interested, please forward or e-mail your resume to:

Mr. Michael T. Wylam
Director - Human Resources
(Email: MTWylam@SweetThing.com)

Sweet Thing Baking Company
115 Commerce Drive
Irvine, CA 18274-2345

Equal Opportunity Employer, M/F

DIANA A. LAWSON

425 Lantern Road
Atlanta, GA 33923

Email: DIALAW@AOL.com

Home: (404) 255-3241
Office: (404) 992-6706

March 8, 2003

Mr. Michael T. Wylam
Director - Human Resources
Sweet Thing Baking Company
115 Commerce Drive
Irvine, CA 18274-2345

Dear Mr. Wylam:

I noted your ad for an Administrative Recruiter in the Sunday edition of *The Orange County Register* with a great deal of interest. I am planning a move to Southern California and would seem to be exceptionally well-qualified for the position you advertised.

I hold a B.A. degree in English from Dickinson College and have spent the last three years as Employment Manager for Sunbeam Corporation, where I have been heavily involved in the successful recruitment of all administrative personnel.

My current assignment requires that I deal effectively with a wide range of staffing sources. These have included college recruiting, employment advertising, employee referral systems, resume databases, alumni associations, professional and trade associations, the Internet, etc.

In the three years that I have been in this position, I have reduced agency fees by 80% (annual savings of $330,000) and reduced the interview-to-hire ratio from 8:1 to 2.5:1. This improved ratio has saved considerable managerial time and returned an estimated $85,000 per year in candidate travel expense.

I am intrinsically motivated to bring continuous improvement to the staffing process and to reduce overall employment costs.

May I have the opportunity of meeting with you during my forthcoming trip to your area? I will be in the area from March 30 to April 15.

Thank you for your consideration, and I look forward to hearing from you shortly.

Sincerely,

Diana A. Lawson

Diana A. Lawson

Enclosure

SANDRA E. LONG

324 White Pine Lane
Wawa, WA 28217   Email: **Selong32@MSN.com**   **Home: (704) 249-8730**
                                                                                    Office: (704) 357-1000

April 20, 2003

Ms. Victoria S. Stratton
Partner
Lloyd Consulting, LLC
Executive Search Consultants
32 Spiral Cliff Road
Winoma, WA 23849-2467

Dear Ms. Stratton:

I was intrigued by your ad for Senior Vice President, Human Resources, in today's edition of the _Seattle Times_ and am enclosing my resume for your consideration. It seems I have some excellent qualifications for this position and my background should be of strong interest to your client.

I am a well-seasoned Human Resources professional with an M.S. degree in Psychology and over 15 years' experience. In my current position as Director of Human Resources for Wellman Corporation, I manage a staff of 35 and provide a full range of Human Resource services to the corporate staff and eight manufacturing plants.

In my earlier assignment as Director of Organization Development, I was heavily involved in organization design and development activities. This included a major redesign and restructuring of the corporate staff. I was also instrumental, as Senior O.D. Consultant, in successfully leading transformation of Wellman's organization culture from a traditional management system to one that is based on socio-technical concepts.

I have always made a point of staying current with new, evolving Human Resource concepts and am quick to seize the opportunity to introduce those having positive effects on productivity. I value being a strong strategic contributor and am known for my innovativeness.

My salary requirements are in the mid-$100K range.

May I have the pleasure of meeting with you to discuss your client's requirements in greater detail? I believe this would prove mutually beneficial.

I appreciate your consideration and look forward to hearing from you.

Sincerely,

Sandra E. Long

Sandra E. Long

Enclosure

PRODUCT DEVELOPMENT ENGINEER

Leading $300 million, non-woven materials manufacturer seeks Product Development Engineer for R&D Group.

Position reports to Product Development Group Leader, with responsibility for the development of new, air-laid materials used as inner and outer barriers for disposable diaper liners and revolutionary, proprietary new absorbent product applications.

Requirements include an advanced degree in Chemical Engineering, Materials Science or Polymer Chemistry with 2-3 years' research experience in non-woven product development. Strong knowledge of polymer chemistry and fiber structures a must. Exposure to super absorbent materials technology a definite plus.

Please forward or e-mail resume, including salary requirements, to:

Dr. Harland P. Richardson
Director-Administrative Services
Technology Group

ABSORBENT STRUCTURES, INC.
105 River Street
Wilmington, DE 47590-5869

(E-mail: HarlandR@AbsorbentStructures.com)

Equal Opportunity Employer

RAYMOND B. KARSON

18 South Wayne Avenue
Summit, NJ 08799   **Email: RayCar@MSN.com**   **Home: (609) 922-6728**
Office: (609) 454-1306

June 9, 2004

Dr. Harland P. Richardson
Director - Administrative Services
Technology Group
Absorbent Structures, Inc.
105 River Street
Wilmington, DE 47590-5869

Dear Dr. Richardson:

I was delighted to see your recent advertisement for a Product Development Engineer in the July issue of _Pulp & Paper Research Newsletter_. It seems my qualifications and interests are a close match for your requirements. I am equally pleased the position is local and would not require my relocation.

Interestingly, I am currently working as a Research Scientist for the Paper Chemicals Division of Hercules, Inc., a major supplier of polymers to the nonwovens industry. My principal accountability is the development of novel, new polymer materials for various nonwovens applications, including super-absorbency. I am thoroughly versed in polymer science and have expert knowledge of fibrous structures (especially nonwoven structures).

I hold a Ph.D. in Chemical Engineering from the University of Delaware and have been awarded 16 U.S. patents relating to polymeric materials and fibrous structures. Ten of these are in the nonwovens field.

I trust that my qualifications will be of interest to you and that we may have the opportunity to meet for the purpose of discussing your requirements in greater detail.

My salary requirements are in the mid-$90K range, however, I am flexible dependent on the specifics of the opportunity.

Thank you for your consideration, and I hope to hear from you shortly.

Very truly yours,

Raymond B. Karson

Raymond B. Karson

Enclosure

DIRECTOR
PROCESS DEVELOPMENT

A Fortune 200, sanitary tissue, personal care and cleaning products company with sales in the $8 billion range, we are the world leader in our field. Our market dominance and continuous success are, in great measure, due to our strong and unending commitment to research and development.

We are in need of a Director of Process Development to lead our research efforts in the area of wet-lay sheet formation process development. This position reports to the Vice President of Technology and is responsible for leading a 20-person department in the development of new papermaking processes, from bench scale through pilot plant study.

This position requires a Ph.D. in Chemical Engineering, Chemistry, or other relevant technical discipline, and a minimum of 10 years' research in papermaking process development. Must be thoroughly knowledgeable in the application of twin-wire sheet forming technology and have led successful development programs in the development of novel papermaking processes.

Excellent interpersonal, communications and leadership skills are also required.

Please forward or e-mail complete resume, along with compensation requirements, to:

Mr. Wayne L. Thompson
Employment Manager – Technology
(E-mail: WLThompson@Barstrom.com)

BARSTROM PAPER COMPANY
750 Paper Mill Road
Green Bay, WI 12837

Equal Opportunity Employer, M/F

WILBERT W. PAULEY, Ph.D.

632 Deer Lake Drive, Green Bay, WI 53302

August 12, 2003

Mr. Wayne L. Thompson
Employment Manager - Technology
Barstrom Paper Company
750 Paper Mill Road
Green Bay, WI 12837

Dear Mr. Thompson:

Your ad for a Director of Process Development in the July issue of the *TAPPI Journal* seems a surprisingly good match for my background. I have a strong interest in the position and am therefore submitting my resume for consideration.

The following qualifications listing highlights the closeness of this match:

- Ph.D. in Chemical Engineering

- Twelve (12) years' papermaking process development (tissue and towel products)

- Expert in twin-wire sheet formation (8 patents)

- Principal scientist in development of revolutionary new transpiration drying process

- Research group leader on highly successful wet lay tissue development process (5 patents)

In my current position as Process Development Group Leader, I have been a successful advocate of several new technology concepts, providing solid evidence of both my leadership and communications skills. My ability to relate to others across the organization has frequently been cited as a key strength.

I would appreciate the opportunity to meet with you and the other members of your Technology Staff to explore how my capabilities might be used to further enhance Barstrom Paper Company's competitive position in the marketplace.

My compensation requirements are in the high $90K range.

Thank you for reviewing my credentials. I look forward to hearing from you.

Sincerely,

Wilbert W. Pauley

Wilbert W. Pauley

Enclosure

ROBERT D. DURAN

120 Rocky Stream Drive
Cincinnati, OH 45292
(513) 762-3177

May 16, 2003

Ms. Eileen M. Lloyd
Director of Human Resources
Global Alloy, Inc.
136 West Nile Avenue
Canton, OH 23958

Dear Ms. Lloyd:

I am forwarding my resume in response to your May 15th ad in the *Canton Daily News* for a Systems Analyst. Comparison of my qualifications with your requirements, as specified in this advertisement, suggests that I would be an excellent candidate for this position.

Qualification Highlights are

- B.S. Degree, Computer Science, Syracuse University

- 2 Years' Experience, Systems Analyst

- Good knowledge of General Ledger Accounting Systems (Accounting Minor at Syracuse)

- Group Leader for Order-Tracking System (a $1.5 Million Systems Project)

My qualifications suggest I would be capable of making an immediate and significant contribution to Global Alloy in its evaluation, selection and successful installation of a general ledger accounting system. Should you agree, I would welcome the opportunity to further explore this opportunity.

Thank you for your consideration, and I look forward to hearing from you.

Very truly yours,

Robert D. Duran

Robert D. Duran

RDD/kaw

Enclosure

122 West Trabuco Canyon Road
Lake Forest, CA 30838

September 20, 2003

Mr. Jonathan W. Parker
Manager of Corporate Employment
Union-Atlantic Insurance, Inc.
135 Grant Plaza
San Diego, CA 23748

Dear Mr. Parker:

I read your September 18th ad in the _Los Angeles Times_ for a Manager of IS with a great deal of interest. From your description, this position seems a good match for my skills and capabilities. I have thus enclosed my resume for your review and evaluation.

According to this advertisement, you are seeking someone with a degree in Computer Science and a minimum of 8 to 10 years' IS experience with an insurance company, bank or other financial institution. I graduated with a B.S. in Computer Science from Ohio State and have over 12 years' IS experience in the insurance industry.

Further, you state that you are seeking a candidate who has successfully managed a sizeable corporate IS group and is intimately familiar with all aspects of providing a high level of systems support to a demanding client base in a fast-paced business environment.

As Manager of IS for Equitable Insurance Company, I direct an 80-employee corporate IS function, providing a full range of systems support to the corporate staff and 125 branch office locations. Our clients are demanding and insist on a high level of support, despite a fast-changing business culture.

Since I live in Lake Forest, a move to San Diego should be rather simple and cost little.

Please review my accomplishments as highlighted on the enclosed resume. Should you agree I am well-qualified for this position, I would look forward to the opportunity of meeting with you personally to further explore my credentials and your specific requirements.

I can be reached at my office on a confidential basis during the day or at my home in the evening. Thank you for your consideration.

Sincerely,

James A. Larkin

James A. Larkin

Enclosure

CHEMICALS BUYER

A world leader in the manufacture and sale of specialty polyurethane foams, our principal customers include major corporations in both the automotive and defense industries.

The Chemicals Buyer will be stationed in the Purchasing Department at our corporate offices in Jacksonville, Florida. This position is responsible for the bulk purchase and delivery of raw material chemicals including resins, TDI, and dyes.

Position requires a degreed buyer with two or more years' experience in chemical purchasing. Must have successfully negotiated large bulk contracts for multi-site manufacturing operations. Should be skilled in the negotiation of long-term contracts at extremely favorable terms.

For consideration, please mail or e-mail your resume and compensation requirements to:

Ms. Mary Ann Gohagen
Director of Materials & Logistics

(E-mail: Gohagen@NationalFoam.com)

National Foam Corporation

**450 Clover Highway, Bldg. 52
Macon, GA 38294**

Equal Opportunity Employer

ORVILLE JACKSON
502 Payton Square, Apt. B-24
Raleigh, NC 80944
(317) 943-2433

July 15, 2003

Ms. Mary Ann Gohagen
Director of Materials & Logistics
National Foam Corporation
450 Clover Highway, Bldg. 52
Macon, GA 38294

Dear Ms. Gohagen:

I would appear to be an excellent candidate for the position of Chemicals Buyer, as advertised by National Foam in the July 12th edition of the *Atlanta Journal*. Please accept the enclosed resume as an indication of my interest in this position.

Comparison of my qualifications with your requirements suggests to me that there is a solid basis for further discussion of this opportunity through a face-to-face interview. Please consider the following qualification highlights:

- B.S. degree, Chemistry Major, Georgia Tech

- Four years' chemical purchasing experience

- Successful negotiation of multi-million dollar chemical contracts for six plant sites

- Excellent reputation as skillful negotiator of long-term contracts at below-market rates

My current annual compensation is $72,000, and I would need an increase in the 10% range to warrant a career move at this time.

I would appreciate the chance to further discuss this opportunity with you and to mutually explore the contributions I might make to your purchasing function.

Thank you for your consideration. I look forward to hearing from you.

Very truly yours,

Orville Jackson

Orville Jackson

Enclosure

VICE PRESIDENT LOGISTICS

A Fortune 150 food manufacturer, we seek a Vice President of Logistics to direct $400 million corporate-wide logistics operation. Functional responsibilities include order entry & tracking, production planning & scheduling, raw materials planning & scheduling, warehousing, distribution and fleet management.

We seek a seasoned logistics executive with 15+ years' experience in all aspects of logistics and materials management. Must have successfully directed large, complex logistics function for major consumer products or foods company. Requires up-to-date applications knowledge of computer systems in the field of materials management.

Position reports to Senior Vice President of Operations and offers a highly competitive compensation package and comprehensive benefits program.

Please submit resume and compensation requirements to:

Ms. Victoria A. Princeton
Senior Vice President, Human Resources

HARBRACE FOODS, INC.
5 Mountain Ridge Road
Nashville, TN 39486

(E-mail: VPrince@Harbrace.com)

An Equal Opportunity Employer

NICHOLAS D. CARBONA

2005 Mission Road, East
St. Louis, MO 23847

Email: NickiCar@HotMail.com

Home: (817) 523-7196
Office: (817) 293-0450

June 22, 2002

Ms. Victoria A. Princeton
Senior Vice President, Human Resources
Harbrace Foods, Inc.
5 Mountain Ridge Road
Nashville, TN 39486

Dear Ms. Princeton:

As specified in Sunday's ad in the *St. Louis Daily News*, you are searching for a Vice President – Logistics. I think review of the enclosed resume could well convince you I am a solid candidate for this position.

Please consider the following highlights of my background:

- Seasoned Logistics Executive with 18 years' experience

- Director of Logistics, Giant Foods Corporation (a $2 billion food and beverage company)

- Manage staff of 60 employees in the day-to-day operation of the corporate logistics function

- Directed the selection and successful installation of a corporate-wide order entry/production scheduling/inventory management computer system ($2 million project)

Over the last five years, I have returned more than $8 million to the business through implementation of several innovative cost-savings initiatives aimed at improving overall logistics efficiencies. Perhaps I could make a similar contribution to Harbrace Foods.

If my background is of interest, I would welcome the opportunity to meet you and other appropriate members of your senior management team for further discussion.

Thank you, and I look forward to hearing from you in the near future.

Sincerely,

Nicholas D. Carbona

Nicholas D. Carbona

Enclosure

RICHARD E. BRENTWORTH

439 Longacre Lane
Harrisburg, PA 17436

Home: (717) 694-8281
Office: (717) 557-1633

June 12, 2003

Human Resources Manager
U.S. Electronics, Inc.
1600 Executive Pavilion
Ridgefield, CT 06898

Dear Sir or Madam:

Enclosed is my resume in response to your recent advertisement in the June 12th edition of the *Harrisburg Patriot* for a Public Affairs Associate. This position sounds exciting and I would welcome the opportunity to discuss it further with you.

As my resume will attest, I appear to have excellent qualifications for this position:

- B.A. degree, Public Affairs, American University

- Two years as Administrative Aid to U.S. Senator Richard Schultz (Considerable public contact requiring poise, maturity and strong communication skills)

- Seasoned, skilled goodwill ambassador in building and maintaining positive public image on wide range of issues

I feel that I have the knowledge, skills and motivation needed to provide strong support to the Manager of Public Affairs in effectively handling both public affairs and legislative affairs matters. My experience in government should also prove a strong asset to this position.

Should you agree that my background is a good match for your requirements, I would welcome the opportunity to meet with you to further explore this excellent opportunity. My salary requirements are in the high $70K range.

Please call me on a confidential basis at my office, or at my home in the evening.

I hope that you will view my qualifications favorably and that I will hear from you shortly. Thank you.

Sincerely,

Richard E. Brentworth

Richard E. Brentworth

Enclosure

COMMUNICATIONS MANAGER

Public Affairs Department of large commercial bank (52 branch offices) seeks communications professional to manage employee publications and internal employee communications program. Will report to the Director of Public Affairs.

We seek degreed professional with five or more years' management experience in internal communications. Must be skilled in the publication of employee newsletters as well as use of various multi-media vehicles for effective internal communications. Strong interpersonal and communications skills are an absolute requirement.

Qualified candidates please e-mail or send complete resume, detailing employment history, to:

Employment Manager

UNIVERSAL SAVINGS BANK
105 Financial Towers, West
New York, NY 19384-0124

(E-mail: Employment@USBank.com)

Equal Opportunity Employer

NICHOLE A. ALLEGRO

132 Prince Street
White Hall, MD 21201

Home: (410) 461-3976
Office: (410) 641-6600

June 1, 2003

Employment Manager
Universal Savings Bank
105 Financial Towers, West
New York, NY 19384-0124

Dear Sir/Madam:

The position of Communications Manager, as advertised in this past Sunday's edition of the *New York Times*, sounds like an exciting opportunity. Please consider the enclosed resume an indication of my interest in this position.

It appears my qualifications are an excellent match for your requirements.

Your advertisement calls for a degreed professional with five or more years' management experience in internal communications. My B.A. degree in English and current position as Corporate Communications Manager for Worldwide Insurance Company should meet your expectations.

Further, your ad states you desire someone skilled in the publication of employee newsletters as well as multi-media used for effective internal communications. I now manage the publication of a monthly corporate newsletter and three regional employee publications. My use of multi-media for internal communications covers the gamut: print media, overhead and rear screen projection, computer generated slides, computer projection, audio and video cassettes, closed circuit TV, satellite transmission, etc.

Both my interpersonal and communications skills are excellent and have always been a major area of strength.

Your opening sounds interesting, and I would welcome the opportunity to learn more during a personal interview at your offices. I hope that you will view my candidacy favorably and I might have the opportunity to further explore your requirements in person during an on-site meeting.

Thank you for your consideration, and I look forward to hearing from you.

Sincerely,

Nichole A. Allegro

Nichole A. Allegro

Enclosure

GERALD D. FINCH
202 Elgin Circle
Fort Worth, TX 60621
(817) 833-5167

August 23, 2004

Mr. Richard K. Brian
Vice President
Search Consultants, Inc.
525 Brainard Blvd.
Lexington, MA 12496

Dear Mr. Brian:

While browsing through the <u>Dallas Star</u> this past Sunday, I came across your advertisement for a Corporate Planning Analyst. Although I am not actively "on the market," this position appears interesting and has prompted me to forward my resume for your consideration.

Review of your client's requirements, as specified in this advertisement, suggests I should be a very viable candidate for this opportunity. Please consider the following:

- *MBA, Wharton School, University of Pennsylvania*

- *Three years as Business Analyst, General Foods Corporation*

- *Undergraduate Degree in Statistics with an Economics Minor*

- *Performed numerous studies and made best recommendations on various business strategies (e.g., buy, sell, merge, expand, contract, diversify, specialize)*

My creativity and resourcefulness in identifying and presenting alternate business options has won the confidence and trust of the senior management team, and I am frequently chosen as the Lead Analyst on major project assignments. Interpersonal and communications skills are two of my major assets.

If you agree that I am well-qualified for this position with your client, I would welcome the chance to meet with you to further explore this opportunity. Since this is a confidential inquiry, I would much prefer being contacted at my home in the evening rather than at my office.

I appreciate your consideration, and look forward to hearing from you at your convenience. Thank you.

Sincerely,

Gerald D. Finch

Gerald D. Finch

Enclosure

MARGUERITE E. HARBSTER

402 Mews Drive, Chattanooga, TN 37202

March 16, 2004

Director of Corporate Employment
Quickburgers, Inc.
1400 Ridge Highway
Norris Lake, TN 64706

Dear Sir or Madam:

I noted your ad for a Corporate Planning Manager in the March 11th edition of *The Tennessean* with considerable interest. This sounds like an excellent opportunity, and I would appear to have the qualifications you seek. Enclosed is my resume for your consideration.

I am a Financial MBA with over 10 years' experience in business planning. Currently, as Business Development and Planning Manager for Best Foods, a $13 billion frozen foods manufacturer, I manage a department of five talented analysts responsible for all business development and planning activities for the corporation.

Our overall charter is to develop and recommend those business plans and strategies required to effectively manage the resources of the business and maximize return on the firm's capital investment. Some key results achieved include:

- Diversification into the frozen concentrate juice market through acquisition of two key companies (Results = 20% ROI in second year)

- Consolidation of Fresh Cut and Greens Divisions into single business (Results = $30 million annual overhead savings)

- Business expansion into Pacific Rim (Results = 60% annual growth rate with excellent profitability)

- Sale of Guerner Dairy Products Division (Results = immediate improvement of 10% to corporate profits)

I have long admired the Quickburgers organization and would greatly appreciate the opportunity to be considered for this position. I feel I am well prepared to take on this assignment and have the knowledge, skills and energy to make a significant contribution to your company.

I would welcome the chance to meet with you and the members of your senior management group to further explore your requirements. I look forward to hearing from you shortly. Thank you.

Sincerely,

Marguerite E. Harbster

Marguerite E. Harbster

Enclosure

ROBERT F. BERNSTEIN
6233 Rose Tree Road
Columbia, MD 21106

MAY 23, 2003

Mr. Phillip E. Zanfagna
Manager of Administrative Employment
Specialty Chemicals, Inc.
635 Third Avenue
New York, NY 23948-4583

Dear Mr. Zanfagna:

While opening the current issue of *Legal Briefs*, I spotted your advertisement for a Patent Attorney. Although I have not been actively looking for a change, your ad did catch my attention. I would like to work in the pharmaceutical industry, and your firm is one of the leaders in which I have interest.

My credentials, as called for in your ad, include a B.S. in Chemistry from the University of Maryland and over two years in the chemical industry as a Patent Attorney. My law degree is from Georgetown University School of Law.

I am currently working in the Corporate Law Division of Ashland Chemical Company, where I am the principal attorney in the patent area. Ashland, as you may know, is a small $30 million manufacturer of intermediate chemicals sold primarily to the pharmaceutical industry. As such, I have had to learn a good deal about pharmaceutical manufacturing processes.

I feel my qualifications are an excellent match for your requirements, and I would appreciate the opportunity to meet with you and the members of your law staff to further discuss your requirements.

Thank you for your consideration. I look forward to hearing from you shortly.

Sincerely,

Robert F. Bernstein

Robert F. Bernstein

Enclosure

234 Kimberly Lane
Albany, NY 16354-1635

November 16, 2002

Box Y-222
The New York Times
New York, NY 10108

Dear Sir or Madam:

I was pleasantly surprised this morning to discover your advertisement for a Senior Vice President and General Counsel in *The New York Times* for two reasons. First, I have recently decided to make a career move. Second, I would appear to be well-suited to your requirements.

As Assistant General Counsel for Bristol Myers-Squibb, a $6 billion pharmaceutical and consumer products company, I report to the General Counsel and have managerial accountability for approximately half the Law Division (30 attorneys). For the last five years, my principal accountability has been to investigate and direct all major litigation work (several cases in the multi-million dollar range) covering a wide range of legal issues from antitrust cases, to consumer liability issues, to class action suits, to patent infringement suits. I am proud to say that I have established a strong "winning" record over the years.

Interestingly, as called for in your ad, I have broad knowledge of corporate law to include both general business and patent law. My career includes five years in the patent area, three years as a legal specialist in human relations, and four years in real estate related areas. This experience, coupled with my litigation background, should make me a very desirable candidate for this position.

My resume is enclosed for your consideration. As requested, my compensation requirements include a base salary in the $175,000 to $200,000 range plus executive bonus.

Should you conclude that I am a viable candidate for this position, I would be pleased to meet with you and the senior members of your management team to further explore my qualifications at your convenience.

Thank you for your consideration, and I look forward to your reply.

Sincerely,

Jerald L. King

Jerald L. King

JLK/se

Enclosure

QUALITY MANAGER

A $400 million manufacturer of copper tubing sold to commercial developers and industrial OEM accounts, we seek a Quality Manager for our copper refining and tube manufacturing facility located in Denver, Colorado. This position reports to the Director of Operations and is responsible for managing the quality function of a 200-employee facility. Reporting to this position are 2 Quality Shift Supervisors and 5 Quality Laboratory Technicians.

The successful candidate will have at least an Associate's degree in science (Engineering Technology, Physics or Chemistry) and a minimum of 3 years' quality supervisory/management experience in the metals refining or manufacturing industry. Must have experience working with engineering and operations personnel to establish the quality standards and inspection & laboratory testing procedures necessary to meet industry standards and customer specifications.

Qualified candidates are encouraged to submit resume and salary requirements to:

Personnel Director
COLORADO TUBE & REFINING, INC.
1500 Rocky Mountain Expressway
Denver, Colorado 15768

(E-mail: Employment@CT&R.com)

An Equal Opportunity Employer

LESLIE M. BAXTER

18 Williston Road
West Orange, NJ 18374

Email: LesBax18@AOL.com

H: (201) 632-5706
O: (212) 449-6000

March 26, 2004

Personnel Director
Colorado Tube & Refining, Inc.
1500 Rocky Mountain Expressway
Denver, CO 15768

Dear Sir or Madam:

This morning's *Newark Star Ledger* contained your advertisement for a Quality Manager, a position in which I am interested. Enclosed please find my resume for consideration.

Your ad states you seek at least an Associate's degree in science and a minimum of three years' quality supervisory or management experience in the metals refining/finishing industry. My qualifications are:

- B.S., Metallurgy, University of Vermont, School of Mining

- Six years' Quality experience, Revere Copper & Brass Co.
  - Two years - Manager of Quality Assurance
  - Four years - Quality Shift Supervisor

Further, as specified in your advertisement, the candidate must have experience working with engineering and operations personnel to establish the quality standards and inspection/laboratory test procedures to meet industry standards and customer specifications. My qualifications include:

- Extensive experience working with Engineering and Operations personnel in all areas related to Quality

- Publication of Quality Inspection and Testing Manual and training of all Quality and Operations personnel in proper inspection and testing methods

I hope that you agree I am well-qualified for your opening and that I will have the chance to further explore this position during a face-to-face interview at your facility. I would welcome this opportunity to discuss your requirements in greater detail.

Thank you for your consideration, and I look forward to your reply.

Sincerely,

Leslie M. Baxter

Leslie M. Baxter

Enclosure

DIRECTOR

QUALITY MANAGEMENT

Leading manufacturer of physical fitness and personal exercise equipment seeks Corporate Director of Quality Management. Position reports directly to the President.

This position will be responsible for leading the design and implementation of a corporate-wide total quality effort based on the concepts and teachings of Dr. Edwards Deming.

We seek Ph.D. in Statistics with 10+ years' experience in total quality field. Must have acted as key architect and principal facilitator of a major SPC-based quality initiative in a multi-plant manufacturing company.

Additionally, the successful candidate must exhibit strong interpersonal, communications and leadership skills. Further, qualified individuals must be able to effectively relate to a wide range of people, from top management to hourly operator.

Highly competitive salary, performance bonus, and comprehensive benefits program are provided.

Send or e-mail resume and cover letter, including compensation requirements, to:

Mr. Allan D. Marks
Vice President, Human Resources

SPORTSFIT, INC.
1000 Kings Blvd., East
Portland, OR 12849

(E-mail: MarksD@SportsFit.com)

LAWRENCE S. SCHAEFFER

22 Ocean View Lane
Santa Barbara, CA 27385

Home: (604) 992-2436
Office: (604) 881-3482

September 10, 2003

Mr. Allan D. Marks
Vice President, Human Resources
SportsFit, Inc.
1000 Kings Blvd., East
Portland, OR 12849

Dear Mr. Marks:

The Classified Section of today's *San Francisco Chronicle* contains your advertisement for Director of Quality Management. My qualifications appear to be an excellent match for this position, so I am enclosing my resume for consideration.

I hold a Ph.D. in Statistics from the University of Illinois and, as called for in your ad, my qualifications include over ten years' experience in the total quality field.

In my current position as Manager of Quality for Stafford, Inc., a $100 million manufacturer of men's clothing, I have successfully facilitated and led the deployment of a company-wide SPC-based quality initiative. This included implementation at three manufacturing sites.

In addition to technical skills, I have strong interpersonal, communications and leadership skills. All of these characteristics were prerequisites to entering my current position and have been critical qualifications needed for effective performance. The success of our current effort provides ample testimony to my strengths in these important areas.

I am a strong Deming advocate and am excited about the opportunity to assume a Director-level position in a company looking for leadership in implementing a corporate-wide total quality effort based upon his teachings. I feel I have much to bring to SportsFit as a candidate and believe I have the overall knowledge and capability necessary to successfully lead your total quality effort.

I encourage your strong consideration of my employment candidacy and hope that we will have the opportunity to meet shortly.

Thank you for your consideration, and I look forward to hearing from you.

Sincerely,

Lawrence S. Schaeffer

Lawrence S. Schaeffer

Enclosure

MANUFACTURING MANAGER

United Foam Technologies is a $75 million manufacturer of reticulated and un-reticulated polyurethane foam sold to acoustical and filtration applications. As a result of excellent growth and increased profitability over the last 3 years, we are now planning a major $15 million capital expansion to begin this year.

We seek a talented, seasoned Manufacturing Manager for our two-plant, 210-employee operation. This position reports to the Executive Vice President and will manage a staff of 10 Manufacturing Shift Supervisors.

The successful candidate will hold a degree in Engineering (prefer Ch.E.) and at least 6 years' manufacturing management experience in the manufacture of polyurethane foam or other polymer-based products. Position requires excellent interpersonal, communications and leadership skills. Prefer some prior plant start-up experience.

Excellent compensation and benefits package is provided.

For consideration, please forward or e-mail complete resume and recent salary history to:

Manager of Human Resources

UNITED FOAM TECHNOLOGIES, INC.
300 Commerce Circle, West
Winston-Salem, NC 26374

(E-mail: HRManager@UnitedFoam.com)

An Equal Opportunity Employer, M/F

SALLY A. SANCHEZ
25 Clearwater Drive
Raleigh, NC 23749
(703) 248-2693

August 2, 2003

Manager of Human Resources
United Foam Technologies, Inc.
300 Commerce Circle, West
Winston-Salem, NC 26374

Dear Sir or Madam:

The position of Manufacturing Manager, as advertised in the August 1st edition of the *Atlanta Journal*, is a surprisingly good match for my qualifications.

Consider the following:

- B.S. in Chemical Engineering, University of Virginia
- 8 years' manufacturing experience - polyurethane foam
- Start-up experience as Plant Manager - Richmond Plant
- Excellent interpersonal, communications and leadership skills

In my current position as Manufacturing Manager for General Foam, I manage an $18 million, three-plant, 75-employee operation engaged in the manufacture of specialty polyurethane foams. During the past three years in this position, key accomplishments have included:

- Reduction of 20% in operating costs. (Annual Savings of $2 million)

- Increased production throughout by 10%. (Annual Value of $1.2 million)

- Reduction of staff by 5%. (Annual savings of $500,000)

Perhaps I could make similar contributions to your firm. I would appreciate the opportunity to meet with you and appropriate members of your executive team to further explore your requirements and my qualifications.

I look forward to your reply and hope we will have the opportunity to meet in the near future. Thank you for your consideration.

Sincerely,

Sally A. Sanchez

Sally A. Sanchez

Enclosure

DIRECTOR OF MANUFACTURING

The Agri Products Division of our $3.5 billion, Oklahoma-based chemical company is looking for a talented Director of Manufacturing for its four-plant, 2,400-employee chemical manufacturing operation. This position reports to the Division President.

We seek a degreed Chemical Engineer with 10+ years' manufacturing experience in agricultural or specialty chemicals. Must demonstrate strong performance record in the profitable management of a sizeable, multi-plant, chemical manufacturing operation. Must also exhibit strong working knowledge of modern manufacturing concepts including JIT, MRP, SPC-based total quality and high-performance work systems.

Conversion of organizational culture from "top down" management operation to a high-performance, socio-technical, systems-based operation will require appropriate management style conducive to successful leadership of this cultural change initiative.

Interested candidates should forward resume and compensation requirements to:

Mr. R. J. Smythe
Vice President, Operations
(RJSmythe@FosterChem.com)

Foster Chemicals, Inc.
915 Prairie View Highway
Oklahoma City, OK 28371

An Equal Opportunity Employer

144

CRAIG B. JESTER

201 Forsythe Avenue
Little Rock, AK 23847

September 2, 2003

Mr. R. J. Smythe
Vice President, Operations
Foster Chemicals, Inc.
915 Prairie View Highway
Oklahoma City, OK 28371

Dear Mr. Smythe:

If, as your September 1st ad in the *Spokesman-Review* suggests, you are looking for a top-flight executive to lead your manufacturing function, you may want to give my credentials careful consideration. I appear a solid match for your requirements.

Please consider the following relevant qualification highlights:

- B.S. in Chemical Engineering, Oklahoma State University

- Total of 13 years' chemical manufacturing experience (8 years in agricultural chemicals)

- Management of $2.6 billion, 4-plant, 1,600-employee, specialty chemicals operation

- First-hand experience with modern manufacturing methodology including JIT, MRP, SPC-based Total Quality

- Extensive training in, and experience with, socio-technical systems approach to management (implemented across all operations)

The enclosed resume details the specifics of my manufacturing management experience and accomplishments.

Should you agree I am a strong candidate, I would welcome the opportunity to meet with you to explore the possible contributions I can make to Foster Chemicals.

My compensation requirements are a base salary in the $125K to $135K range plus bonus.

Thank you for your consideration.

Sincerely,

Craig B. Jester

Craig B. Jester

Enclosure

SCOTT M. BEATTY

132 Clifton Drive, Sacramento, CA 12847   *Phone: (715) 883-9521*

April 5, 2003

Box 188Y
The Orange County Register
200 Irvine Blvd.
Irvine, CA 12738

Dear Sir or Madam:

Today's *Sacramento Daily News* contains your advertisement for a General Manager, along with a brief description of the requirements for this position. My background appears to satisfy your requirements rather well, so I am enclosing my resume for your review and consideration.

I am Group Manufacturing Manager for a $155 million, three-plant division of Westbrook Manufacturing, a leader in the field of precision specialty gauges for the nuclear power industry. I hold a dual degree in Mechanical and Electrical Engineering at the bachelor's level. Evidence of my ability as a solid contributor to business results includes:

- Increased production output by 28% through redesign of manufacturing equipment layout (annual value of $5.6 million)

- Decreased manufacturing costs by 21% over three years through reduction in manpower, improved inventory planning and manufacturing scheduling, and reduction in spare parts inventory ($6.3 million annual savings)

- Implemented total quality program resulting in 96% reduction in scrap and a 98% reduction in customer complaints ($1.4 million annual savings)

These are but a few of the key results I have achieved for employers throughout my manufacturing career. Additional achievements are detailed in the enclosed resume.

As my resume confirms, I have experienced excellent career progression, advancing rapidly to positions of increasing responsibility in the manufacturing field. Additionally, I am credited with having exceptionally strong communications and leadership skills.

My current annual compensation is $135,000. This includes a base salary of $115,000 plus a bonus of $20,000.

I would welcome the opportunity to meet with you for the purpose of exploring contributions I could make to your company.

Thank you for your consideration, and I look forward to your reply.

Sincerely,

Scott M. Beatty

Scott M. Beatty

Enclosure

PRESIDENT & CEO

Internationally known, environmental engineering company located in southeastern U.S. seeks senior executive to head up $250 million firm. Position reports to the Chairman and will have considerable latitude in day-to-day management of this high-growth company.

Successful candidates will possess a degree in engineering, an MBA and at least 10 years' senior management experience in a technology-based consulting firm. Must have demonstrated leadership skills in a fast-growth environment and an excellent track record of profitably growing new businesses through both acquisition and development of new consulting services.

Base salary in the upper $100K range, plus highly attractive bonus program, car and other executive perks in keeping with this level position.

For consideration, please forward your resume in confidence to:

Box 600
THE ATLANTA CONSTITUTION
1000 Peachtree Street, East
Atlanta, GA 19042

DONALD R. SAMSON

122 Glaston Drive
Roanoke Rapids, VA 12738   Email: DSam122@MSN.com   Home: (602) 579-3762
Office: (602) 403-2110

July 16, 2002

Box 600
The Atlanta Constitution
1000 Peachtree Street, East
Atlanta, GA 19042

Dear Sir or Madam:

Your July 16th advertisement in *The Atlanta Constitution* for President & CEO reads like a carbon copy of my credentials. Perhaps we could meet to discuss the possibilities for a successful relationship.

Please consider the following qualifications as they relate to your needs:

- M.S., Environmental Engineering, B.S., Chemical Engineering

- MBA, Finance, Columbia University

- 10 years' total experience - technical consulting
  6 years' experience - environmental consulting
  5 years' senior management - $120 million firm

- Managed rapid-growth business units expanding at annual growth rate of 45%+

- Heavily involved in leading business growth through both acquisition and new business development

In my current position as Executive Vice President of Enviro-Tech, a $120 million environmental engineering consulting firm, I am responsible to the President for the daily operating results of the firm's consulting divisions. I am also a member of the Executive Committee and am considered to be a key force in formulation of both long- and short-range business strategies.

May I suggest we meet to further discuss your requirements? I believe that I am uniquely suited to your needs and have the knowledge and leadership skills necessary to successfully lead your business.

I look forward to hearing from you shortly. Thank you.

Sincerely,

Donald R. Samson

Donald R. Samson

Enclosure

5

Networking Cover Letters

No book on cover letters would be complete without a chapter on the subject of the networking cover letter. Several studies have measured the effectiveness of various job-hunting sources. All agree on one thing—employment networking is, by far, the single most productive source for finding jobs! In fact, studies have consistently shown that somewhere between 63% and 75% of all jobs are actually found through use of the networking process.

WHAT IS EMPLOYMENT NETWORKING?

Employment networking is the process by which the job seeker makes use of personal contacts to find employment. The idea is to use personal contacts to arrange introductions to others who could be influential in helping you with your job search.

The networking process, in principle, works much like the popular chain-letter concept (or cell division theory). It allows you to exponentially expand your own personal contacts by tapping into the social network of others. The process looks something like this:

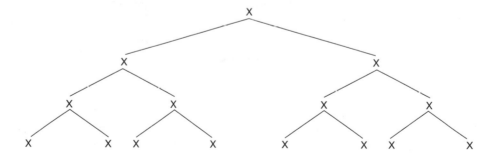

If each contact you make in the chain leads to only two other contacts, the two contacts can quickly multiply to eight contacts, as depicted by the diagram. Thus, by asking each contact to introduce you to two or three other persons who might help you with advice or assistance, it is possible to eventually have several hundred others actively involved in some way with helping your job search.

This extremely powerful technique has demonstrated its effectiveness time and time again!

The purpose of this chapter is to assist you with the composition of effective networking cover letters that can serve as a catalyst to the employment networking process.

PURPOSE OF NETWORKING COVER LETTER

The purpose of the networking cover letter is threefold:

1. Set the stage for a personal introduction.
2. Transmit your resume.
3. Acquaint the contact with your qualifications in advance of your networking phone call or meeting.

The networking cover letter is an important document in helping the networking process to flow smoothly. A well-written cover letter will go a long way toward setting the stage for your networking contacts. If done well, the letter will accomplish the following:

1. Make the person whom you are contacting feel comfortable—willing to open up and share valuable information (that is, job leads and names of key contacts).
2. Provide sufficient information about your qualifications and job-search objectives to allow the contact to make intelligent recommendations to you.
3. Provide sufficient information to allow the contact to intelligently discuss your qualifications and job interests with others.

Conversely, if the cover letter is poorly written, most (if not all) of these benefits will be lost and your targeted contact will not be in a position to provide meaningful help.

A well-written networking cover letter is a critical building block to the success of your job-hunting campaign.

ELEMENTS OF NETWORKING COVER LETTER

The following is a summary of the basic elements of a well-written networking cover letter:

1. Personalized opening paragraph to include:
   a. Name of the person who has referred you.
   b. Nature of your relationship with this person.
   c. Some personal comments (where appropriate).

2. Explanation of how referral came about (optional).
3. Reason for job/career change (optional).
4. Reference to known job opening (if one exists).
5. Indirect networking approach (if no known job exists).
6. Brief summary of qualifications (and reference to enclosed resume).
7. Action statement designed to initiate next action, with networking contact (that is, phone call or personal meeting).
8. Statement of appreciation (that is, a thank you).

The cover letter samples that follow should provide you with an ample array of models from which to choose in tailoring your own networking cover letters.

ROBERT P. GOLDHORN
2606 Highland Avenue
Baton Rouge, LA 70809
(505) 924-6607

October 15, 2003

Mr. Patrick C. Gallagher
National Sales Manager
Whalen Corporation
2015 Bourbon Street
New Orleans, LA 66393

Dear Patrick:

Jerry Currie mentioned your name to me the other day and strongly suggested I contact you. Jerry and I grew up together in Little Rock, Arkansas, and still see each other frequently.

From what Jerry tells me, you are very active as an officer in the American Society of Heating, Refrigeration and Air Conditioning and know a number of sales executives in the industry. As a result, he felt you might be willing to lend me a hand.

Carrier Corporation, my current employer, has recently been sold to United Technologies. United has its own sales organization and will simply fold Carrier's product line into their existing line. Unfortunately, this means that my job, along with the jobs of 25 other Sales Representatives, has been eliminated.

As the enclosed resume shows, I have a B.A. degree in Marketing from Ohio State and have been working as a Sales Representative in the HVAC industry for two years.

Although I certainly would not expect you to be aware of a specific job opportunity for me, I would appreciate it if you could spend an hour or so with me over lunch. I would value any general thoughts and advice you might have concerning my job hunting campaign. Jerry seemed to feel you might be very helpful in this regard.

I will plan to call you next Monday to see when it might be convenient for us to meet. I would very much appreciate your counsel. Thank you.

Sincerely,

Robert P. Goldhorn

Robert P. Goldhorn

Enclosure

621 Edgewater Drive
Glenview, IL 60025

August 15, 2004

Ms. Theresa McDevitt
Executive Director
American Marketing Association
335 Park Avenue
New York, NY 16284

Dear Ms. McDevitt:

As the chief executive officer of the nation's largest professional marketing association, I felt you might be in a position to provide some excellent counsel and advice. I have been an Association member since 1989 and have been active on various regional committees. You may recall that we met briefly over lunch at last year's national meeting in Dallas.

I am currently Vice President of Sales for Zenith Corporation, a $1.5 billion manufacturer of consumer electronics and furniture sold to OEM accounts. In this capacity, I manage an international sales force of over 150 employees and market our products in some 16 countries. A confidential copy of my resume is enclosed for your reference.

Although I have had quite a successful career to date, some recent top management changes at Zenith have caused me to rethink my objectives. As a result, I have decided to make a change and am currently conducting a highly confidential job search. Zenith is unaware of my decision.

I would appreciate if you could spend a few minutes with me on the phone sometime in the next few days. I would value your observations and insight concerning current national trends in the sales profession and how these might impact my job search. Additionally, I would welcome any general thoughts and ideas that you might have regarding my search.

I will plan to call you shortly and look forward to our conversation. In the meantime, I would appreciate any thought that you might give to this matter.

Thank you.

Very truly yours,

Patricia A. Helms

Patricia A. Helms

Enclosure

JAMES R. REARDON

212 Maplewood Road
Cambridge, MA 01742

Email:JRRear212@AOL.com

Home: (617) 575-8859
Office: (617) 630-1130

March 22, 2004

Mr. Bruce J. Reinhardt
Brand Manager
CertainTeed Corporation
570 East Swedesford Road
Wayne, PA 19087

Dear Bruce:

I am writing to you at the suggestion of Roger Dolby, who I understand is a former neighbor of yours. Roger and I were fraternity brothers at Georgia Tech and have stayed in touch over the years.

Recently over dinner, Roger and I were discussing my plans for a career change and your name came up as someone who has a strong professional network in the consumer marketing field. Roger felt, as a result, you might be in a position to assist me.

Bruce, don't get me wrong. I am not expecting that you would have a job for me, nor would I expect that you would be aware of one. Instead, what I am hoping is that you might be willing to share the names of a few good contacts in the consumer marketing field -- persons, like you, who are professionally active and know others in the field. I would also appreciate any general suggestions you might have concerning my job hunting campaign.

I have taken the liberty of enclosing my resume for your reference. In short, I have a B.A. in Business from Georgia Tech and three years' experience as a Market Analyst with Armstrong World Industries. I am seeking a similar position with a major consumer products company, preferably on the East Coast.

I will plan to give you a call sometime during the next week and would hope that you will be able to spend a few minutes with me. I would greatly appreciate your advice and counsel.

Thank you.

Sincerely,

James R. Reardon

James R. Reardon

Enclosure

ELAINE C. MARKESON

722 Peachtree Lane   Home: (404) 454-7665
Atlanta, GA 40434   Office: (404) 231-1900

February 20, 2003

Mr. James M. Borman
President
JMB Controls, Inc.
4335 Main Street
Atlanta, GA 43602

Dear Mr. Borman:

Mike Cullen, a tennis partner and friend, thought it would be a good idea for me to contact you. Mike and I play doubles together at Green Valley Country Club where we also serve on the Board of Directors. I understand from Mike that you're quite a tennis player yourself. He tells me that the last time the two of you met on the courts, you thoroughly humiliated him with your power serve.

During tennis last week, I mentioned to Mike that I would be leaving my position as Director of Marketing for General Precision. General Precision, as you know, is a leading manufacturer of specialty control instrumentation for the chemical process industry.

As President of a major player in the process control field, Mike seemed to feel you would be an excellent person to talk with about my career change. He tells me that you are a very knowledgeable colleague and might have some good advice that would be helpful to my job search. I would very much value your counsel in this regard.

I have enclosed a copy of my resume to facilitate our discussion and would appreciate if you might have a moment to look it over.

Knowing that you likely have a busy schedule, I will contact your secretary early next week to see if we can establish a convenient time for us to talk. I look forward to our conversation and would very much appreciate your advice and counsel.

Thank you.

Sincerely,

Elaine C. Markeson

Elaine C. Markeson

Enclosure

DAVID M. CARMICHAEL

176 Rutherford Way   Home: (208) 535-2708
Boise, ID 83702   Email: DMCarm@MSN.com   Office: (208) 891-1470

July 28, 2003

Mr. John D. Sebera
Director of Manufacturing
Stokley-Van Camp, Inc.
321 North Clark Street
Chicago, IL 60610

Dear Mr. Sebera:

When searching through the Sigma Chi Alumni Directory, I came across your name. (I am a 2000 graduate of the University of Illinois, where I was Vice President of the local Sigma Chi Chapter.) I am writing in hopes you might be in a position to provide me with some advice and assistance.

I have recently elected to make a career change and am looking to find a new position in manufacturing in the food and/or beverage industry. Since graduating with a B.S. in Industrial Engineering in 2000, I have been in manufacturing with Ore-Ida Foods. Most recently, I have been Operations Manager for a 150 employee packaging operation here in Boise.

Although Ore-Ida has been good to me, and I have learned much in the four years since graduation, I do miss the Illinois area. Both my wife and I are from the Greater Chicago area and would love to return, provided I am able to find a position comparable to the one I now hold at Ore-Ida.

Mr. Sebera, as a member of Sigma Chi and as a manufacturing executive with a major food company in the Illinois area, I thought you might be a good person to contact. Although it is unlikely that Stokley-Van Camp would coincidentally be looking for someone with my background, I thought perhaps you might be in a position to introduce me to other manufacturing executives in the Chicago area through whom I might network in finding a suitable opening. In addition, I would greatly appreciate any suggestions you might personally have concerning my job search.

I have taken the liberty of enclosing my resume for your reference. I would very much appreciate if you could spare a few minutes with me on the phone to discuss this matter.

I will call your secretary to see if I can coordinate a time that would be convenient to your schedule.

Thank you for your assistance, and I look forward to talking with you.

Sincerely,

David M. Carmichael

David M. Carmichael

Enclosure

CHERYL A. HUNDLEY
570 Waterloo Road
Rockford, IL 61103
(518) 767-9013

February 23, 2004

Mr. Stephen J. Tomasko
Vice President of Manufacturing
Bowmar Instrument Corporation
4080 North 50th Street, Suite 525
Phoenix, Arizona 85015

Dear Steve:

I am writing to you as a fellow member of the American Manufacturers' Association to request your assistance and advice concerning a career change that I am planning. You may recall that we were introduced by Ann Johnson at the last AMA meeting in Boston and talked at length about implementation of TQC at the operating level. I enjoyed our conversation very much.

Currently, I am Vice President of Operations for Atwood Industries, a $350 million manufacturer of industrial valves. Although a fine company, unfortunately Atwood is family-owned and literally all senior management personnel are members of the Lawler family. This does not bode well for long-term career growth, so I have quietly opted to pursue a career search to find an environment that offers brighter long-term growth prospects.

Steve, although I am not expecting that you will be aware of a specific opening for me, I would very much appreciate the opportunity to talk with you more broadly about my job search campaign. I would certainly value your observations about the general market as well as any ideas you might have that would be helpful to my job hunting approach.

I am enclosing my resume for your review and will plan to give you a call shortly.

By the way, Ann was aware that I would be contacting you and said to say "hello." She mentioned that she was planning to look you up at the AMA meeting next month in San Diego and has some interesting information for you concerning the problem you were having with SPC training of operating personnel.

Steve, I greatly appreciate your help concerning my job search and look forward to our discussion. Thank you.

Very truly yours,

Cheryl A. Hundley

Cheryl A. Hundley

Enclosure

JOSEPH J. HONEYCUTT

901 Eddystone Avenue, Bloomington, MN 55420   *Phone: (715) 243-9772*

August 15, 2003

Ms. Janet Segawa
Engineering Manager
Honeywell, Inc.
95 Edgewood Avenue
New Britain, CT 06051

Dear Ms. Segawa:

Sheri Foster, one of my associates here at The Toro Company, suggested that I contact you. Sheri and I have jointly worked on various engineering projects here at Toro's small motors plant, and have gotten to know each other quite well. She tells me that she had worked two summers for you as a co-op student while attending Hartford University.

Ms. Segawa, after considerable soul-searching, I have decided to make a career change. I have spent the last two years since earning my engineering degree from the University of Minnesota working as a Design Engineer on small motors. Quite frankly, I have not found this work particularly interesting and would much prefer working in the energy-related field on larger equipment such as industrial boilers, heat exchangers and so on.

Sheri tells me you direct an engineering department responsible for design of large boilers and pressure vessels. It is for this reason that she suggested I contact you.

Although you may not have an opening at Honeywell for someone with my credentials, both Sheri and I felt you might have some ideas and suggestions on how to make the transition to the energy-related equipment field. I know, with two years' experience in the design of small motors, this may not be an easy transition for me to make. I would therefore very much value your advice and counsel on this subject.

I have enclosed an informational copy of my resume for your review and would like to give you a call sometime during the next week or so. Perhaps I could prearrange an appropriate time to call through your secretary.

I appreciate your help in this matter and hope that your busy schedule will allow us to talk in the near future.

Sincerely,

Joseph J. Honeycutt

Joseph J. Honeycutt

Enclosure

LINDA S. COLLIER
4153 Sunset Ridge
Cambridge, MA 06017

January 15, 2004

Dr. Neil Loftiss
Senior Vice President - Technology
ACS Industries, Inc.
P.O. Box 7000
Atlanta, GA 40344

Dear Neil:

Bob Price, a close friend of mine, suggested I contact you. Bob and I have adjoining slips at Boston's Old Harbor Marina, where our families have spent several summer weekends sailing together -- I understand that you enjoy a bit of sailing as well.

Last weekend, while at Moon Island, I mentioned to Bob that I have decided to make a career move. Since my background is in senior engineering management, Bob suggested that I contact you to see if you have any thoughts on this matter.

I have an M.S. in Chemical Engineering from Worcester Polytechnic Institute and over 20 years' engineering experience in the chemical process industry. Currently, I am Director of Engineering for Cambrex Corporation's Polymers Division, where I direct a 250-employee central engineering group concerned with the engineering design, installation and start-up of major polymer manufacturing facilities. A copy of my resume is enclosed, providing you with further details of my background

As it turns out, Neil, I will be in Atlanta for two weeks starting February 1. Perhaps, if your schedule would permit, we could meet over dinner. I would welcome the opportunity to discuss my job search with you and would appreciate your general counsel and advice on this matter. I will call your office early next week to see if your schedule will allow us to get together.

Thank you for your help with this matter, Neil, and I look forward to the possibility of meeting with you personally.

Very truly yours,

Linda S. Collier

Linda S. Collier

Enclosure

722 Wakefield Avenue
Cheswick, RI 02895

September 15, 2004

Dr. Elizabeth A. Gilbert
Director of Absorbent Technology
The Procter & Gamble Company
One P&G Plaza, Box 599
Cincinnati, OH 45201

Dear Dr. Gilbert:

Ross Glatzer, a former member of your technical staff, has suggested I contact you. Ross and I are colleagues and have worked together in the Product Development Group of Bonded Fibers, Inc., for the last two years.

Dr. Gilbert, Ross has told me about some of the work that your group has been doing on the development of new, super absorbent systems for use in the development of incontinence diapers. He thought my recent work involving the use of polymer-based gels for super absorbent applications may be of interest to your organization.

I have recently made a decision to leave Bonded Fibers, to seek employment in the Technology Department of a larger corporation, where there is greater emphasis on basic research. It would appear that my background could be an excellent fit with some of the areas on which you are working. I am therefore enclosing a copy of my resume for your review and consideration.

Perhaps, if you do not currently have an opening on your staff, you would be kind enough to share some of your general thoughts and ideas on others in the field of absorbency with whom I should be in contact. I would sincerely welcome your advice and counsel in this regard.

I will plan to call your office next Monday to arrange a convenient time for us to talk. I would greatly appreciate any assistance that you could provide regarding this matter.

Thank you very much.

Sincerely,

Patricia J. Kilpatrick

Patricia J. Kilpatrick

Enclosure

MARTIN S. JOHNSON, Ph.D.

1832 Humming Bird Lane
Trenton, NJ 18273

Home: 609) 391-2359
Office: (609) 575-6722
Email: MSJ1062@AOL.com

June 23, 2003

Mr. Randolph R. Westland
President
Rohm & Haas Corporation
15 Independence Mall
Philadelphia, PA 19119

Dear Randy:

I am writing you at the suggestion of Dave Jackson, a close friend and former classmate at Penn State University. Dave and I were having lunch last Wednesday when I mentioned to him that I was planning to make a career change. He suggested, due to your many contacts in the chemical and related industries, you might be an excellent person to contact concerning my career transition plans.

Randy, I doubt you are aware of a specific job opportunity; however, I would certainly appreciate the chance to talk with you in a more general sense about my job search. Dave tells me you have been very active in various industry associations and, in your current capacity, stay very much on top of what is happening in the industry. Perhaps you would be kind enough to share some of your observations about current industry trends and events that might impact my job search. In any event, I would be most appreciative of any general thoughts and ideas you might have on this subject.

Enclosed is a copy of my resume for your review. Briefly, I have a Ph.D. in Polymer Engineering from Cornell University and over 25 years' research experience in the development of pigments and dyes sold to industrial applications. Most recently, I have been Vice President of Technology for Ashland Chemical Company, responsible for a 50-employee research department in the development of specialty dyes and pigments sold to the paint industry. I am sure you are familiar with our firm.

Randy, I would very much appreciate the opportunity to discuss this matter with you and would sincerely welcome your insights concerning both the industry and my job search.

I will plan to give your office a call next week. I look forward to the opportunity to talk with you personally. Dave has told me a great deal about you.

Thank you for your willingness to be of assistance, and I look forward to our conversation.

Sincerely,

Martin S. Johnson

Martin S. Johnson

Enclosure

DIANE T. RUSSELL

936 Rutledge Avenue
Lincoln, NE 68508

Home: (402) 727-4072
Office: (402) 466-9380

October 14, 2003

Ms. Corinne D. Chapin
Manager of Accounting
Guilford Manufacturing, Inc.
4300 Commerce Square
Pittsburgh, PA 15230

Dear Corinne:

I was talking with Anita Wallgren the other evening, and she suggested that I give you a call. Anita and I have been very active in the local chapter of the National Business Women's Association and have done a lot of scheming together on ways that women might be more assertive in taking control of their careers, and not simply taking what is handed to them.

I guess I have taken our conversations to heart and have now decided that it is time to take charge of my own career. Unfortunately, I find myself in a very male-dominated environment here at Delaney Roe & Company and will need to make a career move if I am going to expect to move ahead with both my career and professional development.

Delaney Roe is a small but high-quality CPA firm located here in Lincoln. They have an excellent reputation and a strong base of medium-sized manufacturing and service clients. I joined them as an Auditor in their Auditing Department two years ago, following receipt of my Accounting degree from the University of Omaha. A copy of my resume is enclosed for your reference.

Corinne, I would like to make the transition from public accounting to a position in manufacturing cost accounting with a medium-to-large manufacturing company, where there would be reasonable expectation for career growth based upon contribution and performance. My current compensation is $55,000 annually.

As an accounting manager for a medium-sized manufacturing firm, Anita seemed to feel you would be an excellent person for me to talk with on this matter. I understand that you successfully made a similar transition a couple of years ago. As a result, you might be in a position to share some of your observations and insights.

I would really appreciate an opportunity to talk with you and would sincerely welcome any overall suggestions that you might have regarding my career search. Perhaps I could call your secretary to arrange for a time that would be convenient to your schedule.

Thank you for your help, Corinne. Anita has told me so much about you, and I really look forward to our conversation.

Sincerely,

Diane T. Russell

Diane T. Russell

Enclosure

EVELYN M. WHITING

415 Woodhaven Drive
Morristown, NJ 08998

Home: (908) 377-5971
Office: (908) 692-2205

May 16, 2004

Mr. Samuel T. Parker
Senior Partner
Arthur Andersen & Company
200 West 57th Street
New York, NY 10026

Dear Sam:

I can see by your new title that things are going rather well for you at Arthur Andersen. Congratulations!

It seems like only yesterday that you and I were talking about your desire to make a move from manufacturing to the world of the "Big 4." I guess the introduction that I arranged for you with Allen Fry was just what you needed to get your career really rolling. I'm glad that things have worked out so well. It's always refreshing to see talented people rise to the top!

Sam, I only wish that my own career was doing as well. Although I really can't complain about having finally "arrived," so to speak, as C.F.O. of Manville Corporation, a recent change in the top management of the business has me concerned. As you know, Allen Dunlap has just been named President here at Manville. Although he is certainly a nice guy, I really don't believe he has the candle power to pull Manville out of the slide it has been experiencing in recent years. As a result, I feel it is time to start actively thinking about a serious career move.

I was wondering what your schedule might look like for lunch sometime in the next week or so. I would really like to get together with you to see what ideas you may have concerning my job search. My decision is highly confidential, of course, and I'm going to need to be most discreet in how I go about doing this. I would welcome your advice and counsel in this regard.

Why don't I give Eileen a call to see what we can set up? I would really appreciate your help on this and look forward to our conversation.

Thanks, Sam, and I look forward to seeing you.

Sincerely,

Evelyn M. Whiting

Evelyn M. Whiting

P.S. I've enclosed a reference copy of my "draft" resume.

74335 East Panama Street
Sacramento, CA 91636

August 29, 2003

Mr. Lawrence D. Robinson
Manager of Financial Planning
Potter & Brumfield, Inc.
324 Ryan Avenue
St. Paul, MN 55164

Dear Larry:

It has been about two years since our last contact, but I'm sure you will remember the work that we did together on the proposed Sinclair merger. At the time, as you will likely recall, I was working as the Senior Analyst for R.L. Polk & Company on the project.

Larry, unfortunately, the current recession has not been kind to Polk & Company. There hasn't exactly been a plethora of merger and acquisition activity lately, and Polk has just announced its decision to cease operations effective October 15. Thus, I am in search of a new career opportunity.

As you may remember, Larry, I hold an MBA from the Wharton School, where my major was Finance. I have been working as a financial analyst for Polk since June of 2000 (following graduation), principally focusing on providing technical support to client management in the financial evaluation of proposed M&A's. I have enclosed an informational copy of my resume to provide you with further details.

I am planning to be in the St. Paul area next week on business and was wondering if we might be able to meet. I would really appreciate some general advice and counsel concerning my job search and thought perhaps we might do this over dinner, provided your schedule will permit. If not, maybe we can compare schedules and find a time that better fits your requirements.

Larry, I really enjoyed working with you on the Sinclair project and came to have a great deal of respect for your knowledge of corporate finance. I would very much value your advice and counsel concerning my career and hope that your schedule will allow us to meet. I will call you later this week to see when we might get together.

Thanks, Larry, for your help in this matter, and I look forward to seeing you again.

Sincerely,

Dennis E. Huebener

Dennis E. Huebener

Enclosure

TIMOTHY P. NOLAN

5226 Diamond Drive, Indianapolis, Indiana 44304   *Phone: (635) 878-3347*

July 31, 2004

Mr. Dale H. Gibbons
Chief Financial Officer
Sharp Electronics
One Presidential Industrial Park
Benton Harbor, MI 49022

Dear Mr. Gibbons:

Your name was given to me by Bob Beavins, President of the Indianapolis Rotary Club. I understand that the two of you were neighbors and used to go sailing together when Bob lived in Benton Harbor. Bob and I have worked together on several Rotary projects over the last three years and have gotten to know one another quite well.

During last Wednesday's Rotary meeting, I mentioned to Bob that I was planning to make a career change. Since I have a strong background in finance, he seemed to feel that I should contact you and suggested that I use his name in doing so.

As summarized on the enclosed resume, I hold an MBA in Finance from the University of Chicago. After nearly 20 years in the Corporate Finance Department of Raytheon, Inc., I moved to Indianapolis as Director of Corporate Finance for Compu-Tech Corporation, a $600 million manufacturer of computer components. This has not proven to be the opportunity initially presented to me by Compu-Tech, and I have thus decided to return to the corporate financial world of the major corporation.

Although it is unlikely that you will be aware of a specific job opportunity for me, I would appreciate the opportunity to meet with you briefly to discuss my career plans and to benefit from any general advice and counsel that you might provide in this regard. It would also be valuable to get your insight concerning the state of the electronics/communications industry and the prospects for developing a fruitful career as a senior financial executive in this industry segment.

Realizing that you have a very busy schedule, I am fully prepared to adjust my own schedule accordingly. Perhaps, if convenient, we might even meet over an early breakfast. In any event, I will plan to call your secretary early next week to see if a convenient time might be worked out.

Mr. Gibbons, I really appreciate your help with my career search and look forward to the prospect of meeting with you personally. Thank you for your help in this matter.

Sincerely,

Timothy P. Nolan

Timothy P. Nolan

Enclosure

ALICE M. COLEMAN
6244 Evergreen Court
Canton, Ohio 44720
(216) 494-8033

September 28, 2003

Mr. J. Brian Schaeffer
Manager of Human Resources
Hoover Company
2000 N. 59th Street
Philadelphia, PA 19132

Dear Mr. Schaeffer:

You may recall that I was a Human Resources Intern at Hoover's Corporate Benefits Department two years ago, while a senior at Drexel University. I certainly appreciated the opportunity to have lunch with you during my internship and valued your overall suggestions concerning my career in the field of Human Resources.

Since I had particularly enjoyed my internship, I was disappointed to learn that there were no entry-level opportunities available in Human Resources at the time of graduation from Drexel last year. Consequently, I took a position as Human Resources Administrator with Warren Manufacturing Company here in Canton. My enclosed resume provides further details regarding this position.

Mr. Schaeffer, I would very much like to return to the Philadelphia area since my family and many of my closest friends reside in the Greater Philadelphia area. I am writing, therefore, to inquire if there are any entry-level openings on your staff for which I might be considered. Down deep, I still have a strong interest in working for Hoover Company.

In the event that there are no appropriate openings available at this time, I was wondering if you or any of your staff members could be of assistance to me in my effort to return to Philadelphia. Perhaps you are aware of others who are looking for someone with my credentials, or persons with whom I should be talking, who could be of assistance in my job search. Any general suggestions you might have in this regard would be greatly appreciated.

I will plan to call you sometime in the next few days and would hope that you might have a few moments to spend with me by phone. I really enjoyed our brief relationship and would value any advice and/or counsel you might be able to provide on this topic.

Thank you very much for your help, and I look forward to speaking with you shortly.

Sincerely,

Alice M. Coleman

Alice M. Coleman

Enclosure

617 Hemlock Lane
Bakersfield, CA 90232

October 30, 2002

Mr. John W. Sullivan
Senior Vice President
Human Resources Department
Rush Industries, Inc.
One Mason Drive
P.O. Box 4000
Los Angeles, CA 90336

Dear Mr. Sullivan:

As Chapter President of the Human Resources Management Association for the Greater Los Angeles Metro Area, you are likely to be aware of senior-level human resources openings from time to time. I am therefore contacting you to see if you might have some suggestions concerning my job search.

I am currently Vice President of Human Resources for Butler Manufacturing, a $1.2 billion, 7,000-employee manufacturer of radar components. In my position, I report to the President of Butler and have worldwide responsibility for direction of the Company's Human Resources function. Details of my qualifications are shown on the enclosed resume.

My decision to leave Butler is highly confidential, and I am therefore being particularly discreet with regard to my job search efforts.

I am seeking a senior-level Human Resources position with a large manufacturing company, where I will be a member of the senior management team and have broad strategic responsibilities for contributing to the overall direction of the business. My compensation requirements are in the $150,000+ range.

I will plan to touch base with you shortly to determine if you are aware of any openings at this level that would be worth my pursuing. Should you not be aware of any appropriate openings, I would sincerely appreciate any thoughts you might have concerning either my resume or my job hunting strategy. Additionally, perhaps you may be aware of other individuals whom I should contact who may be aware of appropriate openings at this level. In any event, I would welcome any ideas and/or assistance you might be able to provide to me.

Thank you very much for your willingness to help, and I look forward to speaking with you personally.

Sincerely,

Nicholas D. Paine

Nicholas D. Paine

Enclosure

MALCOME J. SNOWDEN

145 East 42nd Street
Boston, MA 02120
(617) 353-9217

June 22, 2003

Collette M. Taylor
Director of Corporate Planning
DEP Chemical Corporation
One Liberty Square
Boston, MA 02107

Dear Ms. Taylor:

I have just completed an MBA in Financial Planning at Boston College. Your name was given to me by Jerry Lucas, Vice President of Operations, who suggested I contact you. Mr. Lucas and my father, Donald Snowden, are close personal friends and graduated from Oxford University together.

As my resume shows, I am an honors graduate and hold an undergraduate degree in Mechanical Engineering. My credentials include nearly a year's experience as a Financial Analyst in the Corporate Planning Department of Eaton Corporation, a $700 million British-owned chemical manufacturing company. During this time, I was instrumental in assisting Eaton in the evaluation of several potential acquisition candidates here in the U.S. I left Eaton to complete my final year of graduate study at Boston College.

Mr. Lucas indicated that he thought you might be looking for someone with my credentials for your Corporate Planning Department. If not, however, he felt that you might be willing to provide me with some suggestions and ideas concerning my job search. In particular, he seemed to feel that you might have some ideas about key persons whom I should contact in the chemical industry.

Since I live here in Boston, it would be quite easy for me to come to your office for a meeting at a time that is convenient to you. I would certainly welcome the opportunity for such a meeting and would greatly appreciate your general advice and counsel concerning my job search. I hope that you will have some time in your busy schedule to meet with me.

Recognizing that you may be difficult to reach, I will contact your secretary in an effort to arrange a convenient time for us to get together. I am totally flexible and would be pleased to meet either during or outside normal business hours.

Thank you for your assistance, and I look forward to meeting with you personally.

Sincerely,

Malcome J. Snowden

Malcome J. Snowden

Enclosure

GLORIA A. WALDBRIDGE

11301 Springfield Road
Laurel, Maryland 20708

Home: (301) 688-9259
Office: (301) 779-4018

January 2, 2002

Dr. Craig J. Aiken
Professor & Chairman
Department of Economics
University of Pennsylvania
Wharton School of Business
3400 Spruce Street, 4th Floor
Philadelphia, PA 19104

Dear Dr. Aiken:

I was speaking with Eric Hollingsworth of Fleer Corporation the other day, and he strongly encouraged me to contact you. I understand that you have done extensive consulting for Fleer in the strategic planning area and that you have a number of senior-level contacts in the corporate planning functions of a number of the larger U.S. companies. Consequently, Eric seemed to feel that you might be willing to be of some assistance to me with regard to my current job search.

Dr. Aiken, I hold an MBA in Finance from Columbia University in Finance and have spent the past 25 years in the corporate planning and development field. Currently, I am Senior Vice President - Corporate Planning with Fisher Controls International here in Baltimore.

As the result of some recent changes in senior corporate management, I have elected to confidentially explore a career change. My goal is to find a position as the senior corporate planning officer with a multi-billion dollar, high-technology company. Compensation requirements would be in the $200,000 range.

Eric suggested I contact you, thinking that perhaps you could help me make some key contacts in the industry. I am looking to identify senior-level persons, working either in or with the corporate business development function, through whom I might network in identifying an executive-level position in my field. In particular, I would like to identify individuals who are professionally very active outside their own organizations and who seem to have a number of professional contacts in the business development field. This could include corporate people, business brokers, capital venture people, key bankers, consultants, and the like.

I have enclosed a copy of my resume for your review and reference.

I will plan to call you early next week and would greatly appreciate any thoughts that you might have on this subject.

Thank you for your help in this matter, and I look forward to speaking with you personally.

Sincerely,

Gloria A. Waldbridge

Gloria A. Waldbridge

Enclosure

KARA S. IVERSON

1701 Richards Street
Bridgeview, IL 60310   *Email: KaraIv@AOL.com*   *Home: (312) 398-8664*
                                                                           Office: (312) 227-9786

August 22, 2004

Mr. Kirk D. Foley
Regional Director
Environmental Protection Agency
7400 West 10th Street
Chicago, IL 60455

Dear Mr. Foley:

I am a recent graduate of the University of Chicago with an M.S. degree in Environmental Engineering. Although an excellent student, in view of the current economic conditions, I have been experiencing some difficulty in finding meaningful employment in my field.

In a recent conversation with Senator D'Amato, he suggested I contact you for some assistance. Senator D'Amato and my father, John Slater, were close personal friends and worked for many years on various political committees for the Democratic Party. Specifically, the Senator seemed to feel that you might be willing to help me identify expanding environmental consulting firms who may be looking for someone with my credentials.

If your schedule would permit, I would very much like to come to Chicago to discuss this matter with you directly. Perhaps you might also be kind enough to help me identify key contacts within the field. I would be most grateful for any advice and assistance that you might provide regarding this matter.

I will plan to contact you in a few days to determine if your schedule would allow us to meet. Thank you for your help, and I look forward to the possibility of meeting with you personally.

Sincerely,

Kara S. Iverson

Kara S. Iverson

Enclosure

SHERIFF PATEL
1212 Farady Avenue
Portland, ME 04112
(207) 576-9043

August 22, 2003

Ms. Jane M. Fitzpatrick
Executive Director
National Association of Consumer Affairs
200 Constitution Avenue, NW
Washington, DC 20002

Dear Jane:

Greetings from Portland, Maine! It hardly seems two years ago that we worked so hard together on the national meeting in Dallas. At least our hard work paid off, and the meeting was a major success. I don't envy you the task of having to do that each and every year. It must be exhausting.

Jane, I am writing to ask your assistance with my job search. I have decided that I would like to leave the Portland area in favor of warmer climes and would like to center my search on the southeastern U.S. Both Atlanta and Miami would be of particular interest, however, I am quite flexible in this regard.

As you know, I have been Director of Consumer Affairs for Hanover Industries for the past three years and have over 20 years of experience in the field. I have enclosed a complete copy of my resume for your reference. I might mention that Hanover is totally unaware of my decision, so I would appreciate your handling this inquiry with appropriate sensitivity, which I know you will do.

In your capacity as Executive Director, I know you are contacted from time to time by companies who are looking for senior executives in the Consumer Affairs field. I would appreciate your keeping me in mind for any such inquiries.

Beyond this, however, I would like to discuss my situation with you and seek your advice regarding the best way to conduct my job search. Any thoughts and ideas you might have on this subject would be greatly appreciated. It has been quite some time since I was last in the job market.

I will plan to call you sometime next week and hope that I will be able to catch up with you. (I recall what a busy schedule you have.) In the meantime, perhaps you will have an opportunity to review my resume.

I look forward to our conversation, Jane, and very much appreciate your assistance in this matter. Thank you.

Sincerely,

Sheriff Patel

Sheriff Patel

Enclosure

JANICE M. REILLY
1022 Shilling Circle
Havertown, PA 19244
(713) 356-4193

April 5, 2002

Mr. Martin C. Lang
Vice President & General Counsel
Exxon Corporation
225 East John W. Carpenter
Irving, TX 75062

Dear Mr. Lang:

Jack Brier, one of my colleagues at Swan Oil, suggested that I contact you. I understand that you and Jack began your careers together at DuPont and worked together for nearly 12 years. He speaks very highly of you.

Mr. Lang, I am a corporate attorney and have worked in the Law Division of Swan Oil for two years since my graduation from Harvard Law School in 2000. My area of concentration has been Human Resources law, although I have also been exposed to both patent and antitrust law as well.

I have enclosed a copy of my resume for your reference.

My husband, Jeff, and I have arrived at a mutual decision to relocate to the Dallas area. Jeff has been offered the position of General Manager of DuPont's petrochemicals operation, and I have agreed to attempt to find a suitable position that will provide me with the opportunity for future growth and professional development.

Although you may not be aware of any openings for someone with my credentials, Jack seemed to feel that you might be willing to arrange for some personal introductions to some of your professional colleagues with other corporations in the Dallas area. As you know, it will be important for me to do extensive networking throughout the local legal community if I am going to be successful in locating a suitable career opportunity. Anything that you could do to help me in this regard will be very much appreciated.

I will be in Dallas the week beginning April 22 to do some house hunting and was wondering whether your schedule might allow us to get together for either lunch or dinner. I would greatly appreciate your insights concerning the Dallas legal community as well as any general suggestions you might have concerning my job search. I will give you a call to see if we can coordinate a convenient time to meet.

Jack sends his best and wants to know when the two of you are going deep-sea fishing in the Keys again. He says he's ready whenever you are.

Thank you for your help, and I look forward to meeting with you while in Dallas.

Sincerely,

Janice M. Reilly

Janice M. Reilly

Enclosure

DOMINIC F. GALLO

217 Woodcliffe Avenue, Danbury, CT 80411   *Phone: (203) 877-9014*

November 16, 2003

Ms. Deborah R. Barnes
Senior Partner
Barnes, White & Kauffman
Attorneys at Law
3555 East Euclid Avenue
New York, NY 12201

Dear Deborah:

I really appreciated the help you gave us last year on the Coated Films Antitrust Case. The defense strategy was magnificent and the victory was sweet indeed. Obviously, we've come to have a high regard for you and your colleagues.

Deborah, I am writing to you with regard to a personal and highly confidential matter. As a result of some recent changes here at Tektronix, I have decided to quietly leave my position as General Counsel and seek a similar position with a larger company, preferably in manufacturing. I am therefore enclosing a copy of my resume for your reference.

Knowing of your excellent reputation in the field of antitrust law and some of the key national cases your firm has handled for several major U.S. companies, I thought I would contact you to see if you would be willing to be of some assistance relative to my job search. Specifically, I would appreciate the opportunity to meet with you to discuss this matter personally.

Deborah, I know that you are likely unaware of a specific opening at this time, but I would value your general observations and recommendations concerning my job search strategy. I would appreciate the opportunity to discuss this topic with you on a broader basis. I would personally find such conversation very beneficial. Perhaps we could meet over either lunch or dinner.

I will plan to call your office on Friday of this week to see when you might be available to meet. I look forward to seeing you again and will very much appreciate your assistance on this subject.

Thank you.

Very truly yours,

Dominic F. Gallo

Dominic F. Gallo

DFG/tab

Enclosure

BEVERLY C. MALONE
205 Concord Road
Waterbury, CT 08506
(203) 979-0845

March 23, 2004

Mr. Sean R. Hendricks
Manager of MIS Operations
Pitney Bowes Credit Corporation
5600 Beach Tree Lane
Hartford, CT 06508

Dear Sean:

I am a close, personal friend of Maureen Sullivan, who, I understand, is a colleague of yours at Pitney Bowes. Maureen told me to contact you, feeling that you might be willing to help me with a career change that I am considering. I would be very appreciative of your assistance.

As my enclosed resume shows, I am a 2001 graduate of Columbia University with a B.S. degree in Computer and Information Science and a minor in Accounting. For the past two years, I have been employed as a Programmer/Analyst for Creative Software, a software development firm specializing in the development of computer software with applications in the human resources field. My full resume is enclosed for your reference.

I understand from Maureen that Pitney Bowes has recently undertaken the purchase and installation of a large, broad-based human resources/payroll system. In view of my dual degree and extensive experience with human resources systems, perhaps I may be of some value to you.

Even if you do not have a current opening that is appropriate, I would still like to have the opportunity to meet with you. Perhaps, in exchange for some tips I might be able to pass along regarding the HR systems package you bought, you might be willing to provide me with some valuable suggestions and ideas regarding my job search. This could prove to be a mutually beneficial meeting.

I will plan to call you this Friday to see if we might be able to get together. Right now, the weeks beginning April 5 and April 12 would be convenient for me. I am quite flexible, however, and would be pleased to adjust my schedule to accommodate your needs.

Thank you for your assistance, and I look forward to the opportunity of meeting with you personally.

Sincerely,

Beverly C. Malone

Beverly C. Malone

Enclosure

2166 General Warren Blvd.
King of Prussia, PA 19406

July 23, 2004

Ms. Lynne J. Babcock
President
J.D. Edwards & Company, Inc.
5 Technology Drive
Malvern, PA 19355

Dear Lynne:

How is the General Electric project coming along? I heard through the grapevine that your firm had landed the multi-million dollar installation and start-up project for GE's new general ledger system. Congratulations; that's quite a feather in your cap! It just goes to show that, in the long run, high quality work and talented people "can" win.

Lynne, I am writing to see if you might be willing to help me with a personal matter. I have arrived at the conclusion that, if I want to experience long-term career growth, I am going to need to leave my position as IS Development Manager at Fleming Food Corporation. Although the company has been good to me, capital is tight and the company is beginning to cut several corners -- many in the IS capital projects area. Additionally, future growth prospects for the company look discouraging over the next few years, as the company has lost several of its key patent positions to competition.

I know as a consultant in the IS field, you are well-known and have a number of key contacts. I felt, perhaps, you might be willing to spend a few minutes with me to review my resume and help me with formulation of my job search strategy. Your insights concerning current industry trends and potential opportunity areas could be very beneficial to me at this point in the job hunting process. I would be most appreciative if you could share some of your observations and ideas with me.

How does your calendar look for the week beginning August 8? Would it be possible for you to join me for a long lunch to discuss this matter?

I will call you in the next day or two to see if we can arrange a convenient time to meet. As always, Lynne, I look forward to meeting with you.

Thank you for your willingness to assist me in this matter.

Sincerely,

Edward D. Hughes

Edward D. Hughes

Enclosure

J. MARTIN GILLESPIE

1277 Carnation Drive
Cleveland, Ohio 44115

Home: (216) 833-5221
Office: (216) 632-8735

May 26, 2003

Mr. William D. Lynch
Regional Sales Manager
Transcon Freight Corporation
720 U.S. Highway 1
Erie, PA 17762

Dear Mr. Lynch:

As Regional Sales Manager with Transcon Freight, I am sure you are aware, from time to time, of openings in Distribution Management with some of your customers. Perhaps one of your customers may be in the market for a young, ambitious Shipping Supervisor with strong potential for growth to senior-level management. If so, I may well be an excellent match for their requirements.

As the enclosed resume shows, I hold a B.A. degree in Logistics from the University of Cincinnati and have slightly over two years' experience as a Shipping Supervisor for Goodyear Tire & Rubber at their regional warehouse in Akron. In fact, we have been a major customer of yours and frequently use Transcon for many of our overnight hauls throughout the northeastern United States.

The next time you are in the Cleveland area, I would appreciate the opportunity to meet with you. As a result of your extensive contacts and knowledge of the distribution industry, it would likely be very beneficial to talk with you about my career. I would sincerely appreciate any general thoughts and/or ideas that you feel could be helpful to my career search.

I will call your office shortly to see if your secretary could arrange such a meeting for me. This is, of course, highly confidential, since Goodyear is totally unaware of my decision.

I look forward to the prospects of meeting with you, Mr. Lynch, and would sincerely appreciate your willingness to share ideas and suggestions with me on this topic. Thank you very much.

Sincerely,

J. Martin Gillespie

J. Martin Gillespie

Enclosure

FRANCIS A. VANDERSLICE

2180 Barlow Road
Allentown, PA 16309

Home: (215) 533-8872
Office: (215) 741-2129

September 14, 2003

Ms. Ruth A. Glover
Director of Procurement
Lee Enterprises
111 South Calvert Street
Princeton, NJ 08906

Dear Ruth:

It was nice seeing you again at the National Association of Purchasing Agents meeting in Atlantic City this past spring. Time has really flown, and it hardly seems like six months ago that Gene, you and I were having dinner together at Bally's. That's something we need to do more than just once a year. I have always thoroughly enjoyed our time together.

Unfortunately, Ruth, I find myself needing to face a more serious matter. Keystone Steel has just announced its decision to shut down its furnace operations in Whitehall, which means that as of November 1 I will be "on the street." I only wish they had given us a little more warning of this. With two kids currently in college, things are going to be a bit tight.

I know how active you have been over the years in NAPA and have always admired your ability to get things done through your many personal contacts in the Association. Right now, I wish I were as well "networked" as you. It would certainly come in handy.

If your schedule would permit, I'd like to meet you for lunch sometime in the next week or so. (I'm buying!) I would really appreciate your thoughts and ideas concerning my job search strategy. It has been quite some time since I have had to look for a job, and I'm afraid that my skills are more than just a bit rusty.

As a prelude to our meeting, I am enclosing a "draft" copy of my resume and would appreciate if you could look it over. In addition, I would like to ask you to give some thought to key contacts who are well-connected in the Purchasing field. I need to begin to prepare a list of primary contacts, through whom I can network to identify an appropriate career opportunity.

I hate to dump all of this on you, but I'm really not sure where to turn at the moment. You've always been a great friend, and I know that I can count on you to help me. If you ever need help, I'm sure you already know that I will be there to lend a hand. I hope that you'll never need to face this one. At age 58, it's not going to be easy!

Ruth, I'll call you later this week, and we can work out the details of where and when to meet. Thanks for your help.

Best regards,

Francis A. Vanderslice

Francis A. Vanderslice

Enclosure

PATRICIA A. KAISER

2201 Laurelwood Road   *Home: (609) 776-8139*
Cherry Hill, NJ 08003   *Office: (609) 336-5528*

February 26, 2003

Mr. Clifford D. Breeding
Quality Control Manager
Sinclair Chemical Corporation
32100 Telegraph Road
Houston, TX 75082

Dear Cliff:

I have recently made a decision to leave Teledyne, Inc., where I have been a Quality Engineer for the past two years. When discussing this matter with Ben Watkins the other day, he suggested that I contact you. Ben felt you might be in a position to provide me with some good advice.

Cliff, clearly I am not expecting you will be aware of a job opportunity. Instead, I was hopeful that you might spend a few minutes with me on the phone to share any ideas you might have concerning my job search. In particular, I was hoping that you might suggest some key contacts in the quality field with whom I should be in touch as part of my job search.

Generally, the kinds of people who could prove most beneficial to know are those who are well-connected and appear to know a number of other professionals and managers in the quality field. This might include such persons as professionals and managers working directly in the quality field, vendors who sell products and services to the quality field, consultants, key professors, and so on. I would greatly appreciate if you could help me to identify such persons.

In anticipation of our conversation, I have enclosed a copy of my resume for your review and reference. I would also welcome any suggestions you might have on ways to improve the effectiveness of this document.

Anything you can do to help me with my job search effort will be greatly appreciated. Thank you very much for your help, and I look forward to talking with you.

Sincerely,

Patricia A. Kaiser

Patricia A. Kaiser

Enclosure

DAVID J. PALMER
766 West Rolling Road
Fort Washington, PA 19482
(215) 649-9144

August 22, 2004

Ms. Elaine M. Haggerty
President
The Quality Network, Inc.
6935 Arlington Road
Bethesda, MD 20814

Dear Elaine:

I am writing at the suggestion of Drew Olsen, Vice President of Quality at Nova Electronics Company, who thought perhaps you might be of assistance to me. Drew and I have known each other for several years and are close personal friends.

During lunch with Drew yesterday, he mentioned that you had contacted him to let him know that General Electric was looking for a Director of Total Quality for their Power Products Division in Syracuse. I understand that you had been contacted by a search firm, but Drew couldn't recall which one.

Based upon what Drew has told me about this position, it would appear that I may well be a very good match for their requirements. I have both an undergraduate degree in engineering and a graduate degree in Statistics. I have spent the last 18 years in the quality field, the last four of which have been as Manager of Total Quality for IBM's Industrial Controls Division. I have enclosed a copy of my resume for your reference.

Since I would be interested in pursuing this position, I will plan to give you a call shortly. In the meantime, I would appreciate if you could confidentially pass along a copy of my resume to the search firm that contacted you.

Additionally, Elaine, I would appreciate the opportunity to talk with you more broadly about my job search. Perhaps you may have ideas on key persons with whom I should be in contact during the course of my search. I would certainly welcome any suggestions you may have on this matter.

Thank you for passing my resume along, and I look forward to speaking with you shortly.

Sincerely,

David J. Palmer

David J. Palmer

Enclosure

GAIL M. LEVINE

266 Monticello Street, Chicago, IL 60623

June 12, 2003

Mr. Leo C. Shumaker
Regional Sales Manager
Frontier Chemical Company
100 Enterprise Drive
Houston, TX 75832

Dear Leo:

I am writing to you on a confidential basis to seek your help on a personal matter. As you know, we have had some changes here at Foamex, and I am now reporting to Craig Jenkins, Vice President. I do not view this as a positive move and, as a result, I have elected to make a career change.

Although you are already somewhat familiar with my credentials, I have enclosed a copy of my resume to fill in the gaps. Highlights include a B.S. degree in Chemical Engineering and nearly four years' experience in chemicals procurement. All of this has been with Foamex.

At this point in my career, I am looking for a junior-level management position in the procurement department of a major corporation, where there is the opportunity for long-term career growth. Of course, I would want to remain in the chemical process industry. Compensation requirements are in the low to mid $75,000 range, dependent on opportunity and location.

With your large number of contacts in the procurement field in chemical process related industries, I felt that perhaps you might be aware of someone looking for a candidate with my credentials. Additionally, I would appreciate it if you could share with me the names of some key contacts in the industry with whom it would be a good idea to touch base during the course of my job search.

When you are in the Chicago area next Wednesday, I wonder if you might have some time to spend with me on this topic. Perhaps we might have lunch or dinner together. I would also welcome your overall general advice and counsel on my job search strategy.

I recognize the potential sensitivity of this, so I want to assure you of my utmost confidentiality regarding any help which you provide. Likewise, as I'm sure you can appreciate, my decision to make a career move at this time is also a highly confidential and sensitive matter.

Leo, I will call you to see if we can work something out to meet. Thank you for helping me with this matter.

Sincerely,

Gail M. Levine

Gail M. Levine

Enclosure

STEVEN E. JENNINGS
1020 Farm Springs Road
Spokane, WA 98033

October 21, 2004

Mr. Victor J. Berg
President
Chevron Chemical Company
6001 Bollinger Canyon Road
San Ramon, CA 94583

Dear Vic:

I recently heard from Janet that Bob and you went bone fishing near Catalina and had a great time. This puts me in mind of our great adventure sail fishing two years ago in Key Largo. I can't recall when I've had more fun. You always had a soft touch when it comes to going game fishing. Perhaps I could tempt you away from your work again this year to give it another try -- what do you think?

Speaking of "soft touch," I'm afraid I'm going to need your help. It seems that Chem-Trol Corporation is going to be sold to DuPont, and I'm told that my position as Vice President of Procurement is to be eliminated. So, I thought I had better launch my job search sooner rather than later.

I am enclosing an advance copy of my resume, Vic, and would like to arrange to meet with you as soon as your hectic schedule will permit. I would really appreciate your advice and counsel on my job search.

I will give Sarah a call this Friday to see when we could get together. Could you please alert her to my need to meet with you?

As always, I am indebted to your generosity and look forward to our meeting. Please say "hello" to Janet for me and tell her I "send my love."

Warmest regards,

Steven E. Jennings

Steven E. Jennings

Enclosure

ERIN M. SANDERS
476 Covered Bridge Road
Newtown, PA 18970
(404) 953-2593

July 16, 2003

Mr. Peter H. Woods, Jr.
Director of Marketing
Sanyo Manufacturing Corporation
1440 Ridge Pike
Princeton, NJ 08773

Dear Pete:

You may recall that we met briefly last summer at Hal Linden's 4th of July picnic. During a recent conversation with Hal, he suggested that I contact you and reminded me of our meeting.

Pete, unfortunately, my company, Baird Electronics, has just been sold to Sony Corporation and my services as National Sales Manager are no longer required. Sony is simply folding the Baird product line into their existing sales organization which, of course, is headed by their own Director of Sales & Marketing. Friday will be my last day.

I will be in the Princeton area the week beginning July 28 and would like to meet you for lunch, should your schedule allow. I was hopeful that you might be able to share some thoughts and general advice concerning my job search. Hal says that you are quite knowledgeable of the electronics communications market and might have some general suggestions about possible job hunting strategies. I would sincerely welcome any thoughts you might have on this subject.

By way of preliminary introduction to this topic, I have enclosed a copy of my resume for your review.

I hope your schedule will allow us to get together and that you will be able to join me. I will give you a call early next week to see what your schedule looks like, and we can go from there.

Thanks for your help, and I look forward to having lunch with you.

Sincerely,

Erin M. Sanders

Erin M. Sanders

Enclosure

ALFRED W. CHAPMAN

2206 Maple Leaf Avenue, Lancaster, PA 17762

May 16, 2003

Ms. Claire E. Spencer
Director of Corporate Accounting
Johnson Controls
8700 North Green Bay Avenue
Pittsburgh, PA 15223

Dear Claire:

The other day in a conversation with Shirley Simpson, your name came up. I was telling Shirley about my recent decision to leave my current position as General Ledger Accountant with Lancaster Labs to seek a position offering greater growth potential, when Shirley suggested that I give you a call. I understand the two of you were sorority sisters at Penn State together and still stay in close touch.

Claire, I am certainly not expecting that you will be aware of a job for me. Instead, my interest in talking with you is much broader than that. What I was hoping was that you might have a few minutes to spend with me to review my resume and provide me with some general advice regarding my current job search. I would very much value your counsel.

I will plan to call you shortly to see when might be a convenient time for us to get together. I sincerely appreciate your assistance with my job search and look forward to our discussion.

By the way, Shirley says to say "hello" and to tell you that she is planning to go to the reunion at State College in June. She will give you a call soon to see if the two of you can go together.

Thanks again for your help, and I look forward to the possibility of meeting with you.

Sincerely

Alfred W. Chapman

Alfred W. Chapman

Enclosure

MICHELLE S. GRAYBILL

---

330 N. Guilford Lane
Buffalo, NY 14220

Home: (716) 466-7963
Office: (716) 873-9100

October 3, 2004

Mr. Grant W. Smith
President
Omni Graphics, Inc.
1300 York Avenue
New York, NY 10221

Dear Grant:

Henry Grove and I were talking the other day, and he mentioned that you own and operate a very successful graphics arts firm that does contract work for the Elliott Lewis Agency in consumer goods advertising. As a result, Henry seemed to feel that you might be in a position to assist me, and he suggested that I contact you.

Grant, until Friday of last week, I was the Creative Director for the Duckworth Advertising Agency here in Buffalo. Unfortunately, due to the sudden and unexpected death of Joseph Duckworth, the owner, his widow has elected to close the business. This leaves me in the position of seeking employment.

Rather than bore you with detail in this letter, I have decided to enclose a copy of my resume for your reference. In short, I have a Master's degree in Graphic Arts and over ten years' experience on the creative side of a small family-owned consumer products advertising firm.

Henry seemed to feel that, as a result of your position and contacts in the advertising field, you might be in a position to help me with my job search. Although you may well not be aware of a specific opening, I would very much value spending an hour or so with you to get your overview of the advertising industry and some general suggestions concerning my job search strategy. I sincerely hope you will be able to meet with me.

Grant, I will plan to give you a call later this week to see if we can arrange a mutually agreeable time to meet.

Thank you for your willingness to be of help.

Very truly yours,

Michelle S. Graybill

Michelle S. Graybill

Enclosure

CLYDE M. SULLIVAN
10 Downing Street
New London, Connecticut 06083
(203) 847-5847

March 22, 2003

Mr. Kendall P. Harris
Senior Vice President
Aerochem, Inc.
1600 Marketplace East
Boston, MA 77046

Dear Ken:

I am a neighbor of Ed Meehan and have known Ed for over 15 years. I understand from Ed that the two of you grew up together in the Danbury area and went on to Columbia University together. Ed suggested that I contact you, feeling that perhaps you could be of help to me.

As you are likely aware, La Roche Chemical Corporation is preparing for another sizeable downsizing and will be offering a voluntary separation package to its engineering staff shortly. Since I have been with the company for over 14 years, I expect to receive a fairly attractive financial package as part of this offering. I am giving serious consideration to accepting this offer and seeking career opportunities elsewhere.

Ken, I would very much appreciate the opportunity to meet with you at your convenience to get a better feel for the market. Ed tells me that you have been very active with the American Institute of Chemical Engineers over the years and have a number of key contacts in the chemical industry. Additionally, in your capacity as the head of Aerochem's Engineering & Technology Group, Ed seemed to feel you probably have a fairly good overview of conditions and trends in the chemical industry.

Although I don't expect that you will be aware of specific jobs, I would greatly value your general advice and counsel concerning my job hunting strategy as well any relevant market information that you could provide which might impact my decision to either stay or leave La Roche.

As a prelude to our meeting, I have taken the liberty of enclosing a copy of my resume for your reference. I will plan to call your office this Tuesday to see when it might be convenient for you to meet with me. I sincerely hope that your schedule will permit us to get together in the near future.

Thank you for your help, and I look forward to talking with you on Tuesday.

Sincerely,

Clyde M. Sullivan

Clyde M. Sullivan

Enclosure

MARIA A. CHAVEZ
922 Fitzwater Street
Urbana, IL 60332
(312) 967-8394

June 3, 2003

Mr. C. Benjamin Lutz
Vice President Human Resources
Titan Computer Corporation
400 East Brookline Boulevard
Chicago, IL 60603

Dear Ben:

You are no doubt aware of the current turmoil at LaserTek Computing and the substantial losses that the company has experienced over the last two years. The continuing uncertainty of this situation has caused me to decide to seek employment opportunities elsewhere.

I have long known Ralph Fusco through the Employment Management Association and our time together on the Board and various committees. In recent conversation with Ralph, he suggested that I contact you, feeling that perhaps you could be of some help to me in my job search.

Briefly, I have an MBA from Rutgers University and eight years of Human Resources experience in the electronics industry. For the last five years, I have been Director of Employment for LaserTek Computing. A copy of my resume is enclosed for your reference.

Although you are not likely to be aware of specific job opportunities, Ben, it would be helpful if I could meet with you for an hour or so concerning my job search. I would appreciate the opportunity to discuss my job hunting strategy with you and get the benefit of your counsel concerning my approach. I would also appreciate any ideas or suggestions you might have concerning key persons within the industry with whom I should be in contact for employment networking purposes.

I will plan to contact your secretary early next week to see if your schedule will allow us to get together. I would really appreciate the opportunity to meet with you and hope that you can find some time to share some of your thoughts and ideas with me.

Thank you, and I look forward to the possibility of meeting with you in the near future.

Sincerely,

Maria A. Chavez

Maria A. Chavez

Enclosure

HARVEY B. PRICE
622 Crosby Square
Lake Moses, Washington 99144
Bus: (509) 611-2020 • Res: (509) 331-3670

June 15, 2003

Ms. Gail M. Harris
Director of Marketing
Fine Fabrics, Inc.
1135 Sussex Blvd.
Spokane, WA 99413

Dear Gail:

Last evening following our weekly tennis match, I mentioned to Frank Brady that I was considering leaving my position as National Sales Manager for Kennedy Textiles here in Spokane. Frank mentioned that he knew you quite well and strongly suggested that I give you a call. He felt, as a result of your position at Fine Fabrics, you might have some ideas or suggestions for me about my job hunting campaign.

Gail, if it wouldn't be too much of an imposition, I would really appreciate the opportunity to meet with you. Perhaps we could get together over lunch in the next week or so. I would very much value hearing your views on the state of the wholesale industry and with whom I should be in contact for networking purposes as I begin my job search.

Since you will need to know more about my background and overall qualifications, I have enclosed a copy of my resume for your reference. Your review and suggestions concerning ways in which this resume might be improved would also be very additive to my employment campaign.

I would very much appreciate the opportunity to meet with you and hope that your schedule will allow us to get together shortly. I will call you on Thursday to check your schedule and see if we can arrange a convenient time to meet.

Gail, thank you for helping me with this matter, and I look forward to meeting you.

Sincerely,

Harvey B. Price

Harvey B. Price

Enclosure

6

The Resume Letter

The resume letter is a cross between a cover letter and the resume. First, it is a cover letter, serving to transmit your credentials to the employer. Second, it is actually a replacement for the resume itself and is designed to provide a brief synopsis of your employment qualifications. The resume letter both communicates and markets your qualifications to prospective employers.

The popularity and use of the resume letter have grown over the last few years, and more and more of these letters are showing up in corporate and search firm mailboxes. The proliferation of these documents, however, is not necessarily a testimonial to their effectiveness as a job-hunting technique. There appears to be no concrete evidence that they are any more effective than the conventional cover letter and resume combination. In fact, some survey data suggest just the opposite.

ADVANTAGES OF RESUME LETTER

Proponents of the resume letter argue there are certain advantages realized by the job seeker when using the resume letter in place of the conventional cover letter and resume. The advantages typically cited by these individuals are as follows:

1. A one-page letter format is more likely to be read than a two- or three-page letter and resume format.

2. If well-written, the resume letter provides just enough information to stimulate curiosity and interest, but not too much information that would cause the candidate to be "screened out" from further hiring consideration.

3. Providing only limited information in a resume letter can create enough interest to lead to a telephone interview with a prospective employer. This event provides candidates with an opportunity to "sell themselves"—an opportunity not normally afforded to those sending a "complete" resume.

4. Because managers and employment professionals often receive such a huge volume of unsolicited, multipage resumes, one-page resume letters are appreciated.

5. Where cost is a consideration, use of a one-page resume letter versus a multipage cover letter and resume packet, can be considerably cheaper. Use of the one-page format allows the job hunter to send a much larger mailing for the same or lower cost.

On the surface, these arguments sound good. However, you need to consider the disadvantages of the resume letter before accepting it as a job-search panacea and adopting it as the centerpiece of the job-hunting campaign.

DISADVANTAGES OF RESUME LETTER

The truth of the matter is that many employment professionals view the resume letter with a certain amount of disdain. Disadvantages cited by this group include the following:

1. Resume letters usually contain insufficient information to effectively determine if the candidate is truly qualified for a given opening.
2. Lack of detailed information does not allow the employer to determine the "degree" of qualification for a given position.
3. Insufficient information prevents proper comparison with other qualified candidates, placing the author of the cover letter at considerable competitive disadvantage.
4. Busy managers and employment professionals are loathe to pick up the telephone and call a candidate simply to determine whether he or she has the basic qualifications for the opening. Most don't want to risk wasting the time, only to find out the candidate is unqualified.
5. Users of resume letters may sometimes be viewed as *suspicious* or *deceptive* by employers. Why else would they not furnish a complete accounting of their qualifications and experience in the form of a standard resume format?
6. Some employers may also view users of resume letters as lazy—unwilling to commit the necessary time and effort to prepare a proper resume document.

The SHRM survey (nearly 600 employment professionals) mentioned in earlier chapters shows the great bulk of staffing professionals (87%) look negatively on those applicants who send only a cover letter. Although, the resume letter is a slightly different document than the standard employer cover letter, it appears this statistic does not bode particularly well for candidates who elect not to send a full resume.

The list of disadvantages is a convincing one and might well discourage job seekers from using the resume letter as part of their job-hunting strategy at all. Since there is no direct survey data available that is specific to resume letters, it appears that "time is still out" on the true effectiveness of this approach. So, one cannot simply write it off as totally worthless.

The resume letter is likely to be more effective when mailed directly to functional managers (those who have the openings) rather than to the employment manager or human resources department. These functional managers normally receive far fewer resumes and cover letters than busy employment professionals. Therefore, your resume letter has a better chance of being read and generating a positive response.

In the final analysis, using the resume letter in a broad-based survey campaign to functional managers at several hundred companies might be worth trying. All you have to lose is the postage! Certainly, it would be less expensive than to mail a full resume and letter packet (that is, paper costs would triple). This would allow you to reach a much larger group of employers at far less cost.

COMPONENTS OF EFFECTIVE RESUME LETTER

If a resume letter is going to succeed, it must be well designed and well written. Review of the following sample resume letters will reveal there are certain key components that increase the effectiveness of these letters as a job-hunting tool. These elements are:

1. Statement of employment interest.
2. Statement of job search objective (that is, position sought).
3. Broad summary of relevant qualifications, including:
   a. Educational credentials.
   b. Job related experience.
   c. Important traits and characteristics.
4. Summary of important job-relevant accomplishments.
5. Salary and geographical requirements (optional).
6. Request for employer action.
7. Specific contact instructions (optional).
8. Statement of appreciation for consideration.

The sample resume letters that follow will assist you in creating an effective resume letter of your own. Review them carefully before deciding on the format that will best suit your specific needs.

BRUCE D. HAWKINS

151 Pilgrim Avenue
Warwick, RI 02888   *E-mail: Bruce151@MSN.com*   *Home: (401) 727-9165*
                                                                              Office: (401) 999-0300

August 22, 2003

Mr. Vernon M. Olson
Senior Vice President
Sales & Marketing
Electronic Data Systems Corporation
330 Engineering Drive
Marietta, GA 30067

Dear Mr. Olson:

I am a highly successful National Sales Manager with an excellent, well-documented record of accomplishment in the sale of electronic components to O.E.M. accounts in the defense industry. Highlights of my background include:

- B.S. and M.S. degrees in Electrical Engineering

- Direct 80-person international salesforce, selling direct and through distributors

- Products include microwave antennae and receiver components for military guidance and tracking systems

Key accomplishments:

- Revamped field sales organization and market approach, driving sales from $25 million to $126 million in only four years

- Successfully introduced six new products -- all achieving sales volume that exceeded business plan objectives (two by more than 50%)

- Reduced cost of sales by 18% over two-year period

I am seeking an executive sales position with a high-tech, electronics parts manufacturer, with opportunity to manage both sales and marketing functions. The position could be at either the corporate or division level. Compensation requirements are a minimum base salary of $125,000 plus significant incentive compensation potential.

If my credentials interest you, I can be reached at the numbers or e-mail address shown on the above letterhead. I look forward to hearing from you.

Thank you for your consideration.

Sincerely,

Bruce D. Hawkins

Bruce D. Hawkins

1595 Springhill Road
Overland Park, KS 66202
June 10, 2004

Mr. John F. Franklin
President
Triad Consulting, Inc.
410 Mission Plaza
Miami, FL 66202

Dear Mr. Franklin:

I am a talented, energetic Sales Representative with three years' experience in the sale of paper converting equipment to the paper industry. My accomplishments include:

- Sales Representative of the Year, Southeast Region, 2003

- Three consecutive years of record sales volume increase:

    - 2003 15% increase ($100 million to $125 million)
    - 2002 33% increase ($ 75 million to $100 million)
    - 2001 25% increase ($ 60 million to $ 75 million)

- Landed company's largest single account ever ($12 million)

Products sold include winders, slitters, folders, wrappers, carton machines, and sealing equipment. Current territory covers Florida, Georgia, North Carolina, South Carolina, and Alabama. Sales are direct and through manufacturer representatives.

I am ready for my first sales management position and am seeking a district or regional management position with a firm offering the opportunity for future advancement into senior management.

Current compensation includes a base salary of $70,000 plus bonus ($20,000 in 2003).

Please contact me should any of your clients be looking for someone with my credentials. My home phone is (913) 877-9306, and I will be pleased to furnish a complete resume as appropriate.

I look forward to hearing from you.

Sincerely,

Constance A. Radcliff

Constance A. Radcliff

CLAUDINE B. HARRIS

612 Ledge Road   **Home: (314) 233-9176**
St. Louis, MO 63164   **ClaudHar@MSN.com**   **Office: (314) 757-2100**

January 14, 2005

Mr. David C. Burgey
Vice President Marketing
Kingston Corporation
3776 South High Street
Columbus, OH 43207

Dear Mr. Burgey:

If you are currently looking for an accomplished Brand Manager with a strong consumer products background, you may want to take a look at my credentials. I have the education, experience and track record that clearly demonstrate my ability to play a vital role in the successful undertaking of major marketing initiatives.

My qualifications include:

- M.B.A. in Marketing, Harvard University, 2002
- Three years' marketing brand management for a Fortune 100, consumer products company

My accomplishments include:

- Led successful introduction of major, new body shampoo line, achieving 15% market penetration ($300 million sales) in two years
- Successfully repositioned failing detergent line, increasing sales by 325% in three-year period
- Generated highly creative advertising theme for stagnant product line, accounting for increase in market share of 28 points

I possess the knowledge, creativity, and drive to bring similar accomplishments to Kingston Corporation, given the right support and opportunity. In exchange, I am looking for the opportunity to achieve accelerated compensation and career growth commensurate with the level of my contribution to the company.

Should you wish to explore how I might help your organization get its marketing program into high gear, I would welcome the opportunity to meet with you.

Since my search is confidential, I would appreciate if you would contact me at my home or via email. An answering machine will take your message, and I can be back to you by the following business day. Thank you for your consideration.

Sincerely,

Claudine B. Harris

Claudine B. Harris

DOREEN E. BAXTER
2004 Orlando Blvd.
Jacksonville, FL 08034-2837
Phone: (726) 544-8891   Email: DorBax20@MSN.com

October 20, 2004

Mr. Donald F. Preston
President
Euro Marketing, Inc.
1400 Commerce Drive, East
Orlando, FL 33607

Dear Mr. Preston:

I am seeking an equity position as a Partner in a small to medium-sized marketing consulting firm. I have strong credentials and can bring the Fortune 100 marketing perspective to an emerging consulting practice.

Consider the following credentials:

- M.B.A. in Marketing, University of Southern California

- 25 years' Marketing experience as follows:

    - 5 years, Vice President Marketing, Clorox Corporation
    - 3 years, Director of Marketing, Scott Paper Company
    - 5 years, Senior Brand Manager, Campbell Soup Company
    - 3 years, Brand Manager, Campbell Soup Company
    - 2 years, Brand Manager, Kraft Foods
    - 2 years, Associate Brand Manager, Kraft Foods
    - 3 years, Senior Marketing Analyst, Kraft Foods
    - 2 years, Market Research Analyst, Kraft Foods

My years of experience are replete with marketing success stories, with major contributions easily documented in all marketing categories from new product introductions to brand repositioning, through successful national roll-out of numerous product lines.

At this stage in my career, I would like to step back from the corporate political environment and once again focus my energies on the technical side of Marketing. I have considerable experience and numerous contacts that could well benefit a growing consulting firm that is looking to penetrate the major consumer product companies.

If what I have told you is of interest, let me suggest we meet to further explore the strengths that I could bring to your firm. Confidential calls can be placed to my office at the number shown above. I look forward to hearing from you and thank you for your consideration.

Sincerely,

Doreen E. Baxter

Doreen E. Baxter

WENDY L. REED
126 Rolling Green Drive
Columbia, MD 19283
(410) 775-0982
WER126@AOL.com

January 22, 2004

Mr. Brandon B. Smythe
Operations Manager
National Packaging, Inc
422 Wayne Circle
Nashville, TN 58947

Dear Mr. Smythe:

I am an energetic, motivated project engineer looking for an opportunity to break into operations management. Specifically, I am looking for a position as Shift Supervisor or Department Manager in a papermaking or converting operation, where I can put my technical knowledge and leadership skills to work.

The following is a short synopsis of my credentials:

- B.S., Mechanical Engineering, University of Maryland
- One year as Senior Project Engineer - Papermaking
- Two years as Project Engineer - Converting

I have strong interpersonal and leadership skills. These have been clearly demonstrated through my on-campus activities while at the University of Maryland. Evidence of these skills includes:

- Sorority President, Senior Year
- Sorority Vice President, Junior Year
- Sorority Pledge Master, Sophomore Year
- Captain, Women's Varsity Swim Team, Senior Year
- President, American Society of Mechanical Engineers

I am now ready to make my career transition from technical support to line manufacturing management. With my combination of strong technical and leadership skills, coupled with considerable energy and enthusiasm, I feel my new employer will experience an outstanding return on their investment.

I hope you have heard enough to stimulate your interest and that I will hear from you shortly. Thank you for your consideration.

Very truly yours,

Wendy L. Reed

Wendy L. Reed

RHONDA F. HARBSTER

---

800 Morningstar Road, Cedar Rapids, Iowa 14256   Phone: (254) 257-9827

June 16, 2003

Mr. Arnold. F. Barrimore
Vice President, Operations
Meade Corporation
1 Meade Plaza
Dayton, OH 28374

Dear Mr. Barrimore:

I am currently working in Operations Management with Bowater Corporation, a Meade competitor, and have decided to make a career change. I am seeking a senior-level operations management position at the division or corporate level, with multi-plant P&L responsibility.

In my current position as General Manager of Bowater's Cedar Rapids Plant, I am responsible for overall management of a 1,500-employee papermaking and converting facility involved in the manufacture of sanitary tissue and household paper products. This mill includes four twin-wire Yankee tissue machines and full converting facilities.

Educationally, my qualifications include a B.S. degree in Chemical Engineering from the Drexel University and an M.B.A. from Rutgers. I have had considerable management training while with Bowater, including several courses related to the development and utilization of "high performance work teams." Additionally, I have been thoroughly schooled in modern manufacturing systems and concepts including SPC-based total quality, MRP, JIT, and so on.

My experience at Bowater has thoroughly prepared me to assume senior-level management responsibilities in a major pulp and paper company. During my 15 years with the company, I have advanced through a series of functional assignments including engineering, engineering management, human resources management, distribution management and operations management. I have held key operations management positions in both papermaking and converting.

Throughout my career, I have continuously maintained the highest performance ratings, and my operating units have always rated in the top 10% in productivity and efficiency within the Paper Division. During the last two years, the Cedar Rapids Plant, for example, has been rated the best overall performing plant site and has received Bowater's coveted "Plant of the Year" award.

Mr. Barrimore, should you have a need for a senior-level manufacturing executive with a strong record of achievement in the manufacture of consumer paper products, I would welcome the opportunity to meet with you. I can be reached during evening hours at my home phone (216) 949-1593.

Thank you for your consideration.

Sincerely,

Rhonda F. Harbster

Rhonda F. Harbster

DAVID P. SAMSON
325 River View Drive
New Orleans, LA 63749

September 12, 2002

Mr. William T. Carter
Manager – Engineering Services
Web Technologies, Inc.
200 Wilson Industrial Park
Madison, WI 27384

Dear Mr. Carter:

I am an energetic, hard-working Control Systems Engineer with two years' plant project engineering experience in the design, installation and start-up of computer control systems on high-speed web handling equipment. My background and experience would appear to be well-suited to your web handling equipment, technical consulting practice.

Highlights of my qualifications include:

- B.S. Degree, Systems Engineering, University of Utah

- Two years, Control Systems Engineering, Kimberly-Clark Corporation, Neenah Plant

- Engineering design, installation, start-up of $5 million TDC 3000 Control System Project (Paper Machine and Converting Equipment)

  Project included engineering of complete system -- computers, instrumentation and related control devices

I am seeking a senior consulting or supervisory level position providing consulting services to clients in the specification and selection of control systems. My compensation requirements are in the high $70,000 range.

Should you be in the market for a strong control-systems professional or manager, I would welcome the opportunity to meet with you. I can be reached at my office on a confidential basis during business hours. My office phone is (615) 873-4592.

Thank you for your consideration, and I look forward to hearing from you.

Sincerely,

David P. Samson

David P. Samson

820 General Howe Drive
West Chester, PA 19382

May 15, 2004

Dr. Samuel B. Wexler
Vice President, Engineering
General Dynamics Corporation
35 Santa Marguerita Way
El Segundo, CA 26378

Dear Dr. Wexler:

If you are in search of a senior-level engineering executive to manage your company's central engineering department, you may want to give serious consideration to my candidacy.

Highlights of my qualifications include:

- B.S., M.S., Electrical Engineering, University of Vermont

- M.B.A., North Carolina State University

- 25 years' Engineering/Engineering Management experience as follows:

  - 5 years, Vice President Engineering, Lockheed Martin Aerospace
  - 4 years, Director of Engineering, Lockheed Martin Aerospace
  - 6 years, Manager, Corporate Engineering, Hughes Aircraft
  - 4 years, Department Manager, Electronics Design, Hughes Aircraft
  - 6 years, Engineer/Senior Project Engineer, Boeing Corporation

In my current position as Vice President of Engineering for Lockheed Martin Aerospace, I manage an 800-employee central engineering group responsible for all capital project work throughout the company. This includes engineering and start-up of complete manufacturing plants, installation of new manufacturing and assembly lines in existing facilities and major rebuild work. Annual capital budget is in the $1 to $1.5 billion range.

I have established an excellent reputation based on the quality and quantity of capital project work completed. Most of the engineering project work performed under my direction has come in at or below budget, and I enjoy an excellent reputation for meeting key project deadlines. Additionally, I am respected by subordinates as a "demanding but fair leader."

My decision to leave Lockheed Martin is a confidential one, and the company is totally unaware of my present job search. Current compensation is in the high $100K range.

Should you have an interest in my credentials, I would be pleased to meet with you to explore the contributions that I could make to your engineering efforts. My home phone number is (610) 696-4072. Thank you.

Sincerely,

Wilson B. Harris

Wilson B. Harris

BARBARA A. SANDLER, Ph.D.

502 Green Tree Court
New Hope, PA 19384   BarSan@MSN.com   **Home: (203) 436-6267**
                                                        Office: (203) 827-3200

December 18, 2003

Dr. Mathew B. Dawkins
Research Director
Bristol Meyers Squibb
20 Lawrenceville Road
Lawrenceville, NJ 28395

Dear Dr. Dawkins:

I am a Research Investigator with over ten years' experience in antiviral related research. I am aware of the exciting work your company is doing in this area and would be interested in exploring opportunities as a member of your research staff.

My credentials include a Ph.D. in Molecular Biology from the New York University, where I spent six years in a post-doctoral program doing basic research related to virology. Since then I have been employed as a research scientist in the Antiviral Department of Johnson & Johnson., where I have conducted independent research studies to define unique viral targets for antiviral intervention and have collaborated with other research groups in the design and development of novel antiviral agents.

The basic research budget at J&J has recently been cut, and several of my research projects have been adversely affected. Consequently, I am looking for a company that has a strong commitment to its basic research programs and is heavily funding projects in the antiviral area. Bristol Meyers Squibb appears to fit these criteria rather well.

My current annual compensation is $75,000, and I would require an offer in at least the high $70,000 range in order to give serious consideration to a career move.

Should you have an interest in my credentials, Dr. Dawkins, I would welcome the opportunity to meet with you to discuss contributions I might make to your research programs and objectives. I can be reached at my home during the evening or, on a confidential basis, at my office during the day. I also check my email messages several times daily.

Thank you for considering me, and I look forward to hearing from you.

Very truly yours,

Barbara A. Sandler, Ph.D.

Barbara A. Sandler, Ph.D.

Donovan H. Ohr, Ph.D.

915 Birch Road
Reston, VA 23219

DonOhr@AOL.com

Home: (714) 552-4927
Office: (714) 772-1927

March 14, 2004

Mr. Wilson P. Good
Vice President, Research & Development
Wharton Chemical Company, Inc.
22 Independence Mall
Philadelphia, PA 19283

Dear Mr. Good:

I recently heard a rumor you might be looking for a Director of Research at your corporate offices in Philadelphia. If true, I wanted to let you know of my strong interest in this position.

As Vice President of Technology for Bio Industries, I direct all research activities of a 75-employee research center engaged in biotechnology research. During my five years in this capacity, we have successfully developed and launched over 30 new products, accounting for a dramatic increase in annual sales volume ($75 million to $220 million). Additionally, we have another 22 patents pending, which could more than double current sales over the next two years.

Educationally, I hold a Ph.D. in Biochemistry from the University of Washington and an M.B.A. in Finance & Marketing from Pepperdine University. I have over 20 years of biotechnology research experience, starting as a Research Scientist and advancing through several professional and managerial assignments to my current senior management position.

A strong team player, I have developed an excellent reputation for working closely with the marketing and manufacturing functions to rapidly develop and successfully commercialize a number of new products. My interpersonal and communications skills are quite good.

I have long admired the work that Wharton Chemical has been doing in the field of cancer and virology research and would welcome the opportunity to join your senior management team as Director of your research effort.

Should you be interested in pursuing my candidacy, I would be pleased to meet with you at your convenience. I can be reached at the phone numbers shown on the above letterhead.

Thank you for your consideration.

Sincerely,

Donovan H. Ohr, Ph.D.

Donovan H. Ohr, Ph.D.

MICHAEL T. MCCARTNEY

1600 Lake Drive, South
Madison, WI 28395

MikeMCC@MSN.com

Home: (614) 591-7806
Office: (614) 228-8484

April 28, 2003

Ms. Mary Jane Lowell
Director of Corporate Accounting
Mitchell Electronics Corporation
3800 Technology Circle
Seattle, WA 21905

Dear Ms. Lowell:

If you are looking for a strong General Ledger Accountant for a corporate or division-level assignment, you may want to consider giving me a call.

I hold a B.S. degree in Accounting from the University of Illinois and have four years' accounting experience with the Prudential Insurance Company. Previous experience includes two years as an Auditor with Coopers Price Waterhouse, during which time I received my C.P.A.

Currently, I am Senior Accountant in Prudential's Corporate Accounting Department. In this capacity, I report to the Manager of Corporate Accounting and have functional accountability for reconciliation of general ledger account balances, preparation of monthly profit and loss statements, compliance with external filing requirements and related financial analyses.

I am thoroughly familiar with all aspects of general ledger accounting and associated standard accounting procedures. I am also well-versed in both federal and state filing requirements and work closely with the Corporate Tax Department in preparation of federal, state and local tax returns.

As you may be aware, Prudential has recently undertaken a massive downsizing effort, reducing the size of its corporate staff by nearly 35%. My position is one of several hundred the company has elected to eliminate.

If you are looking for someone with my credentials, or if you are aware of any openings outside of Mitchell Electronics, I would appreciate hearing from you.

Thank you for your time and consideration.

Sincerely,

Michael T. McCartney

Michael T. McCartney

CAROLYN A. MANCHESTER
120 DESERT RANCH DRIVE
AUSTIN, TX 39273
(435) 779-2347
Email: CarMan12@MSN.com

July, 20, 2004

Mr. Walter S. Rathbone
Chief Financial Officer
Armstrong World Industries
100 Armstrong Place
Lancaster, PA 19384

Dear Mr. Rathbone:

I have recently decided to make a career change and am currently looking for a senior accounting management position (director or vice presidential level) with a major consumer products company. The position I seek could be at either the corporate or division level.

Should you be seeking a solid, highly-competent accounting executive for a key management position at Armstrong, you may want to consider my credentials as follow:

- MBA, University of Chicago (Major: Finance)
- BS, Ohio State University (Major: Accounting)
- CPA, Commonwealth of Pennsylvania

- Key Accounting Management experience includes:

  - 3 years, Division Controller, Johnson & Johnson
  - 2 years, Director Corporate Accounting, Johnson & Johnson
  - 3 years, Manager Corporate Accounting, Johnson & Johnson
  - 2 years, Tax Manager, Campbell Soup
  - 2 years, Auditing Manager, Campbell Soup
  - 3 years, Plant Accountant, Campbell Soup
  - 2 years, Senior Manufacturing Accountant, Campbell Soup
  - 1 year, Manufacturing Cost Accountant, Campbell Soup
  - 2 years, Auditor, Coopers & Lybrand

My rapid advancement and career progression should provide solid evidence of my professional capability. Additionally, I am known for being a charismatic leader with excellent interpersonal and communication skills.

Should this brief summary of my qualifications be of interest, I would be delighted to meet with you to explore opportunities with your company. I sincerely appreciate your consideration and look forward to your reply.

Sincerely,

Carolyn A. Manchester

Carolyn A. Manchester

Jennifer A. Martinez
20 Mountain Ridge Road
Boulder, CO 98052

February 18, 2004

Mr. Raymond T. Stalworth
Director of Corporate Finance
Campbell Soup Company
One Campbell Way
Camden, NJ 12839

Dear Mr. Stalworth:

If you are looking to add a young, experienced Financial Analyst to your staff with strong merger and acquisition analysis background, please take a close look at my credentials. I have the education and experience that could prove beneficial to your M&A goals.

Please consider the following credentials:

- MBA in Finance, Wharton School, University of Pennsylvania

- BS in Chemical Engineering, University of Michigan

- Four years' merger and acquisition analysis – National Consumer Brands Company, Corporate Development Department.

Key accomplishments include:

- Analysis of 15 acquisition candidates

- Development of acquisition analysis computer model allowing faster, more accurate evaluation of acquisition candidates

- Recommendations resulted in purchase of four companies, all now meeting or exceeding ROI projections

If my qualifications interest you, I would appreciate the opportunity to further explore how my capabilities might complement your efforts through a personal interview.

I can be reached at my office (206) 477-3909 during the day, or at my home (206) 428-4392 during evening hours. Thank you for your consideration.

Sincerely,

Jennifer A. Martinez

Jennifer A. Martinez

VICTORIA W. BENSON
422 Brainard Court, Apartment 12-B
Mobile, AL 74103

Phone: (205) 674-2938   *Email: VicBen422@MSN.com*

June 28, 2003

Mr. Kenneth B. Langford
President
Langford-Jones Consultants, LLC
1515 Peachtree Street, SW
Atlanta, GA 28395

Dear Mr. Langford:

Should you be conducting a search for a senior consultant with strong multifunctional management background and proven consulting experience, I would be interested in discussing how my experience and competencies might fit your needs.

In my last assignment, Vice President of Direct Phone Operations at Marsdale Investment Company, I had the opportunity to further expand my many years of consulting experience in the design and implementation of financial and business planning processes. My MBA in Finance from Dartmouth's Tuck School proved a firm foundation upon which to build and deliver several important contributions.

The remainder of my experience has been split between operations and business planning. My undergraduate engineering training (Rochester Institute of Technology) has provided me with the vital analytical and problem-solving tools to quickly identify critical factors underlying business issues and to design and implement those programs required to improve operations significantly. Over 70% of my experience has involved international operations.

I am seeking a senior finance or business development consulting role with a small to medium sized consulting firm. Target client industries could include petrochemical, chemical, biotech, high tech, transportation and specialty materials.

My qualifications and experience are strongly multifunctional, providing the breadth and practical understanding essential to building client trust and confidence, with particular credibility in dynamic growth or turnaround environments. I would like to talk with you concerning my credentials, as well as the key contacts and value I can bring to the table. I will call you shortly to see if we can arrange a convenient time to meet.

Sincerely,

Victoria W. Benson

Victoria W. Benson

24 Willow Lane
Raleigh, NC 17524

November 22, 2005

Mr. Alfred T. Finnerty
Corporate Planning Manager
Ashland Oil Company
Two Ashland Plaza
Dallas, TX 77252

Dear Mr. Finnerty:

As Corporate Planning Manager for a leading petrochemical company, perhaps you are looking for a talented and accomplished financial analyst to join your staff. As a Senior Planning Analyst for one of Asland's key competitors, my background could be of particular interest to you.

My overall qualifications include an MBA in Finance from Kansas State University and four years' experience in the Corporate Planning Department of Westland Chemical Company, where I have worked as both a Planning Analyst and Senior Planning Analyst. Key projects include:

- Analysis and long-range forecast of business growth potential for Lubricants Division

- Study and recommendations concerning feasibility of entering the mass retail market for motor oils

- Economic feasibility study and recommendations on proposed multi-million dollar expansion of the Philadelphia Refinery

- Numerous "what if" studies to support Executive Committee in preparation of corporate long-range strategies and business plans

I am consistently rated at the highest level during performance evaluations and am recognized as a top contributor within the planning department. Additionally, I am frequently assigned as Lead Senior Analyst on most company key planning projects.

Should you wish to discuss my qualifications further, I can be reached at (715) 353-9144 during the day or (715) 559-3176 during the evening.

I appreciate your consideration and look forward to hearing from you.

Sincerely,

Nelson N. Kennard

Nelson N. Kennard

CHRISTOPHER T. BEATTY

102 Canyon Lane
Tustin Ranch, CA 54738

Email: ChrisB102@MSN.com

Home: (949) 399-7149
Office: (949) 687-4210

June 26, 2004

Mr. James A. Reardon
Executive Vice President
Federal Paperboard Company, Inc.
515 River Rock Drive
Portland, OR 38294

Dear Mr. Reardon:

I have been watching the rapid growth of Federal Paperboard over the last five years and have been quite impressed with the company's strategic leadership. Your strategic positioning in the value-added segment of the market has done much to move you ahead of competition. Your record is impressive and speaks for itself!

Two years ago, I left my position as Director of Corporate Planning with Packaging Corporation of America to accept the position of Vice President of Corporate Planning with Transamerica Corporation. Although I have done well in this assignment, I miss the excitement of working for a manufacturing company. Consequently, I have decided to return to the packaging industry and am seeking a senior-level position in corporate planning.

My credentials include an MBA in Finance from Stanford University and over 18 years' experience in corporate planning and finance. Most of my career has been with PCA, where I advanced rapidly through a series of financial and planning assignments. This included two years as Director of Corporate Finance and nearly four years as Director of Corporate Planning.

Some key accomplishments at PCA have included:

- Successful acquisition of six corrugated mills, doubling the company's corrugated manufacturing capacity.

- Led company's entry into the laminated bleached board market, now the most profitable segment of the business (28% of net profits).

- Sale of company's Folding Box Division to Champion International Corporation for $960 million (considered a major strategic coup).

Perhaps you may be looking for a strong executive to head your planning function. If so, I would welcome the opportunity to meet with you to further explore my qualifications and to discuss the possible contribution I could make to your company.

Thank you for your consideration.

Sincerely,

Christopher T. Beatty

Christopher T. Beatty

BRANDON H. WHITTING

225 Parker Drive, SE
College Park, Maryland 18274

Home: (301) 937-4706
Office: (301) 543-0900

May 9, 2002

Mr. Michael W. Sanford
President & CEO
The Sanford Group, LLC.
1832 Connecticut Avenue
Washington, DC 20006

Dear Mr. Sanford:

As key lobbyist for the tobacco industry, you could well have some interest in my background as a Legislative Affairs Specialist for your firm. Please consider my credentials.

I am a 1998 graduate of the University of Maryland with a Master's degree in Government & Politics. For the past two years, I have been employed as a Legislative Representative for the National Tobacco Manufacturer's Association at their headquarters in Washington. In this position, I am responsible for representing the interests of the Association with respect to pending legislative matters and working with coalitions of various lobbying interests to influence legislation having impact on the industry.

Some of my key accomplishments have included the following:

- Was the key catalyst in combining the efforts of 12 different associations and lobbying firms to defeat the *No Smoking on Public Conveyance Bill*.

- Worked with top aids of Senator Harrison's office to re-word the Clean Air Act to minimize its negative effect on the Tobacco Industry.

Prior to this, I worked for two years as a Legislative Assistant to Senator John Thornton. In this capacity, I was heavily involved in researching and drafting key legislation that the Senator wished to support. In addition, I worked behind the scenes to solicit senatorial support and align a variety of political forces in support of sponsored legislation.

I feel my political connections, coupled with my knowledge of the inner workings of the political system, could prove quite valuable to a lobbying consulting firm such as yours.

Should you agree, I would welcome the opportunity to meet with you to explore how I might fit into your consulting practice. Thank you for your consideration, and I look forward to hearing from you.

Sincerely,

Brandon H. Whitting

Brandon H. Whitting

KEVIN C. CHO

120 W. Church Street
Orange, NJ 19087

Home: (585) 337-5276
Office: (585) 878-3304

March 12, 2004

Ms. Catherine B. Fairchild
President
Career Visions, LLP.
640 Irvine Blvd.
Irvine, CA 98305

Dear Ms. Fairchild:

I did not wish to bore you by sending yet another unsolicited resume to your attention. Instead, this letter will serve to briefly highlight my credentials so that you can ascertain the appropriateness of my qualifications for current search assignments on which you may now be working.

I hold an M.A. in English (communications emphasis) from Northwestern University and have over 20 years' experience in the field of Public Affairs. A brief summary of recent experience follows:

- 5 years - Vice President Public Affairs, Micro Computers
- 3 years - Director of Communications, CB Technologies
- 4 years - Manager Employee Communications, Sun Company

The current economic turmoil at Micro Computers, coupled with the frequent turnover of its senior management team and general uncertainty, have prompted my decision to seek employment in a more stable environment.

I am seeking a senior executive-level position in Public Affairs in a medium-sized or major corporation that has demonstrated a solid record of growth and financial performance. My compensation requirements are in the $125,000 to $135,000 range, and I am open to geographic relocation.

Should you have a client in need of a talented, seasoned Public Affairs executive, I would welcome your call. Should our conversation lead to further interest, I would be pleased to furnish a full resume at that time.

Thank you for considering my qualifications, and I look forward to hearing from you.

Sincerely,

Kevin C. Cho

Kevin C. Cho

DIANE P. LEHMAN
1600 Cornell Avenue
Cherry Hill, NJ 18724
(609) 576-9415

April 2, 2004

Mr. Michael Feinberg, Esq.
Feinberg, Finkle & Rothchild
Attorneys at Law
120 South 12th Street
Philadelphia, PA 19063

Dear Mr. Feinberg:

A recent graduate of the University of Pennsylvania Law School with over four years' previous experience as Law Clerk for the corporate legal department of Campbell Soup Company, I am now ready for my first assignment as a practicing attorney. Please consider my credentials as follow:

- J.D., University of Pennsylvania School of Law (with Honors)

- B.S., Political Science, Swarthmore College (*cum laude*)

- Four years, Law Clerk, Campbell Soup Company

During my employment with Campbell Soup, I worked in two areas of law. Three of these years were spent doing patent research and handling a portion of the patent filing process under the direction of Mary Ann Claxton, Corporate Patent Attorney. The remaining year was spent providing research and support to Harold Schultz in consumer litigation.

My educational background and work experience with Campbell Soup have provided me with a solid foundation upon which to build a successful career in the practice of law. I would like to begin my career with a private law practice such as yours where, through hard work and contribution to the firm, I might eventually have the opportunity to advance to the position of Partner.

Should you be looking for a well-educated, ambitious young attorney to join your firm, I would welcome the opportunity to meet with you to explore this possibility. With my drive and motivation to succeed, I know that I can make a substantive contribution to the firm.

My home telephone number is listed above and my email address is DiLehman@MSN.com. Thank you for your consideration, and I look forward to hearing from you.

Sincerely,

Diane P. Lehman

Diane P. Lehman

WALTER K. KAUFMAN

184 Valley Ridge Drive
Utica, NY 12395

January 8, 2004

Ms. Linda A. Weston
President
The Weston Group
202 Great Valley Parkway
Great Valley Corporate Center
Malvern, PA 19355

Dear Ms. Weston:

Should one of your client corporations be searching for a Vice President and General Counsel, you may want to consider my credentials. Some highlights of my qualifications are:

- LL.B., University of Virginia, School of Law.

- Direct 25-person corporate law department for $15 billion electronic components manufacturer.

- Over 20 years' corporate law experience with major corporations.

In my current position as General Counsel for Reiker Electronics, I report to the President and am responsible for all legal matters pertaining to the operation of this $16 billion corporation. Some major achievements include:

- Out-of-court settlement of a $120 million government contract lawsuit for $18 million.

- Won major antitrust case which would have required divestiture of most profitable division.

- Defeated major class action suit that would have cost government contracts valued at $85 million.

My current annual compensation is $345,000 ($225,000 base salary plus $120,000 executive bonus). I qualify for stock options and am provided with a company car.

Should you feel one of your clients may have an interest in my background, I would welcome the opportunity to talk with you. I can be reached at my office phone, (305) 991-8507. Thank you.

Sincerely,

Walter K. Kaufman

Walter K. Kaufman

P. BARRY SNEIDER

18 Prairie Lane, Houston, TX 27385   Email: PBS1832@HotMail.com   Phone: (716) 897-4432

April 16, 2004

Mr. Dirk K. Dickson
IS Manager
Hartwell Corporation
8506 Industrial Square, East
Cleveland, 21776

Dear Mr. Dickson:

I recently learned you are installing a Novello System 200 at your Cleveland corporate offices. I have been Project Manager for the successful installation and start-up of this same system at Slater Chemical Corporation here in Houston and could be a valuable asset to your project.

Some highlights of my career include:

- B.S., Computer Science, University of Washington

- Five years IS experience with Slater Chemical as follow:

1 year	-	Project Manager, Novello System 200
2 years	-	Senior Analyst, Human Resource Systems
1 year	-	Analyst, Accounting Systems
1 year	-	Programmer/Analyst General Support

For your general information, Novello System 200 poses a particular challenge since certain key documentation is missing. Additionally, some of the functionality which Novello lists in its product specification is simply nonfunctional and needs debugging.

If you are interested in hiring an experienced Novello System 200 Project Leader who has been on the "bleeding edge of technology," you may want to give me a call. I can probably save you many weeks of installation time and much stress and frustration (not to mention money).

Should you wish to contact me, I can be reached at (306) 868-7419. Thank you for your consideration.

Sincerely,

P. Barry Sneider

P. Barry Sneider

DARYL C. SAIKERS

1432 Welborne Drive, Durham, SC 32901
DRSumm@Rockwell.com

June 16, 2004

Mr. William P. Wagner
Senior Vice President
Corporate Administration
Vortex, Inc.
1830 Quaker Square
Columbus, OH 22204

Dear Mr. Wagner:

Some recent management changes at Rockwell International have prompted my decision to seek a career change. This decision is highly confidential, and senior management is unaware of my intention. I am seeking a senior, executive-level position in IS management with a high-technology manufacturer.

Highlights of my qualifications are as follows:

- MBA, University of Connecticut

- B.S., Computer Science, Georgia Tech

- 26 years' IS experience with most recent career assignments as follows:
  - 5 years - Vice President, IS, Rockwell International
  - 2 years - Director of IS, Rockwell International
  - 2 years - Manager IS Operation, IBM Corporation
  - 1 year - Manager Client Services, IBM Corporation

In my current position as Vice President of IS at Rockwell, I report to the Executive Vice President - Administration, and have responsibility for directing a 240-person IS function with operating and administrative budget of $43 million. Some key accomplishments include:

- Successful installation and start-up of $20 million, corporatewide general ledger system.

- Successful installation and start-up of $18 million, corporatewide, totally integrated order entry and tracking/production and inventory scheduling/purchasing system.

I enjoy an excellent reputation for timely, cost-effective delivery of state-of-the-art IS systems that have greatly enhanced management decision making and increased overall company productivity. Excellent references are readily available.

Should you have an interest, I can be reached at (407) 768-3306 or at the above e-mail address. Thank you for your consideration.

Sincerely,

Daryl C. Saikers

Daryl C. Saikers

BARBARA A. HAYNES
405 North High Street
West Chester, Pennsylvania 19382

October 25, 2003

Mr. Thomas C. Wilcox
Manager of Distribution
SmithKline Beecham
Broad & Chestnut Streets
Philadelphia, PA 19101

Dear Mr. Wilcox:

I recently read about SmithKline's plan to construct a 900,000 square foot manufacturing and distribution facility in Montgomery County. This suggests that you may shortly be in need of experienced distribution professionals. If so, please consider my qualifications as follows:

- B.A., Business Administration, Temple University

- Four years' distribution center management experience as follows:

  - 1 year - Distribution Center Manager
    Campbell Soup Company, Camden, NJ

  - 2 years - Warehouse Supervisor
    Campbell Soup Company, Camden, NJ

  - 1 year - Shipping Expeditor
    Scott Paper Company, Chester, PA

Some key contributions have included:

- Conducted one-year carrier study, resulting in major shift from truck to rail shipments (18% annual cost savings)

- Improved production efficiency by 12% and decreased product damage by 65% through reconfiguration of high-volume product storage pattern

I have been watching SmithKline's impressive growth and would very much like to have the chance to explore employment opportunities with your firm. I am hopeful, therefore, that I will be hearing from you.

I can be reached at (610) 527-3615. Thank you for your consideration.

Sincerely,

Barbara A. Haynes

Barbara A. Haynes

140 White Pine Road
Westfield, NJ 14758

August 20, 2003

Mr. Barton W. Bosworth
Executive Vice President
General Foods Corporation
41 Commerce Place
White Plains, NY 14637

Dear Mr. Bosworth:

If you are searching for a strong candidate for a senior-level Logistics management position with your corporate staff or one of your larger divisions, you are likely to be interested in my credentials. My background in the consumer goods industry, coupled with significant contributions in the Logistics area, may well be of benefit.

Currently Corporate Director of Logistics for Lever Brothers, I direct a staff of 65 employees responsible for worldwide management of all Logistics activities of this $2.8 billion consumer products manufacturer. Functional responsibility includes production planning & scheduling, purchasing, scheduling & management of raw materials inventories, warehousing, and distribution management.

My credentials include a Master's degree in Distribution Management from the University of Tennessee and a B.S. degree in Industrial Engineering from Purdue University. I have 22 years' experience in Logistics and Logistics management at two major companies (Lever Brothers and Procter & Gamble) and have held a series of progressively responsible management positions in most functional areas comprising the Logistics area.

I have a legacy of being a major contributor to overall business strategy and have implemented numerous programs resulting in millions of dollars of savings to my employers. I also enjoy an excellent reputation as a manager and leader of people. Interpersonal and communication skills are considered exceptionally strong.

I would appreciate the opportunity to meet with you and other appropriate members of your senior management team to explore how I might fit into your organization and to discuss the potential contributions I could make to your company. Should you wish to explore this matter, I can be reached at (516) 247-2155.

Thank you for your consideration.

Sincerely,

Michelle A. Fagen

Michelle A. Fagen

MARY JOE HAMPTON

614 Amish Trail   Home: (717) 497-8728
Lancaster, PA 19872   Email: MJHamp@MSN.com   Office: (717) 310-6776

November 22, 2003

Mr. David R. Jameson
Director of Quality
Johnson & Johnson Consumer Products, Inc.
Grandview Road
Skillman, NJ 08558

Dear Mr. Jameson:

If you are currently in the market for an outstanding candidate for a Quality management position at
Johnson & Johnson, you will likely have an interest in my qualifications. Please consider the following
credentials:

- B.S. Degree, Industrial Engineering, Rutgers University

- Certified Quality Engineer, A.S.Q.C., 2000

- Regional Chairperson, A.S.Q.C., Northeast Region (two years)

- Total Quality Education:
    - Dr. G. Edwards Deming Seminar, 1998
    - Crosby Quality College Graduate, 1998
    - Statistical Process Control, University of Tennessee, 1997
    - Introduction to Quality Statistics, 1997

- Six years' Quality Management experience with The Gillette Company as follows:
    - 2 years -   Quality Manager, Framingham Plant
    - 2 years -   Assistant Quality Manager, Corporate Offices
    - 2 years -   Quality Associate, Corporate Offices

I have a strong background in the design and implementation of SPC-based total quality initiatives in
chemical process manufacturing facilities, and am up-to-date with most leading-edge quality concepts and
approaches. My knowledge and leadership have earned me solid recognition at Gillette as well as
external recognition by A.S.Q.C., where I now serve as Chairperson for the Northeast Region.

Should you have an interest in my background and wish to further explore my candidacy, I can be
reached at the phone numbers or email shown above. Thank you for your consideration.

Sincerely,

Mary Joe Hampton

Mary Joe Hampton

SHARON W. LEWIS

204 Canyon View Ridge, Lake Forest, CA 27384   Phone: (949) 552-7197

July 24, 2003

Mr. Kenneth G. Taylor
Vice President of Operations
Colorado Copper & Brass, Inc.
325 Mountain Blvd.
Denver, CO 53095

Dear Mr. Taylor:

I am a well-seasoned, knowledgeable Quality executive with strong background in the metal refining and processing industry. I am seeking a Director or Vice President level position with a progressive metals industry manufacturer looking for strong leadership in the Quality area.
Please consider my credentials:

- B.S. Degree, Metallurgical Engineering, Colorado State University

- Certified Quality Engineer, American Society of Quality Control

- 16 years' experience in the quality field, which includes:

4 years	-	Director of Quality, Colorado Brass, Inc.
5 years	-	Manager of Quality, Colorado Brass, Inc.
2 years	-	Quality Supervisor, Waldon Tube Company
1 year	-	Senior Quality Engineer, Waldon Tube Company
3 years	-	Quality Engineer, Powers Pipe Company

In my current position as Director of Quality at Colorado Brass, I led the design and corporate-wide implementation of a highly successful SPC-based total quality program. This included the corporate staff and the company's three manufacturing facilities.

The program is credited with reducing customer complaints by 92% and lowering scrap by more than 80%. Estimated annual savings of this initiative is $15 to $20 million annually.

Should you have an interest in my qualifications, please feel free to contact me at my office, (414) 234-6026.

Thank you for your consideration, and I look forward to hearing from you.

Sincerely,

Sharon W. Lewis

Sharon W. Lewis

QUENTIN D. BROOME
1525 Lansing Road
Detroit, MI 48105

June 25, 2005

Ms. Barbara S. Lim
Director of Procurement
Glaxo Inc.
Five Moore Drive
Research Triangle Park, NC 27709

Dear Ms. Lim:

As you are probably aware, the Warner-Lambert Company has recently announced a cutback in the size of its Ann Arbor workforce by some 1,800 employees. My position, unfortunately, was one of many that have been eliminated by the company.

Should you be in the market for a talented, energetic Procurement Manager for either a corporate or division-level assignment, I would welcome the opportunity to speak with you. A brief summary of my qualifications follows:

- B.S., Chemical Engineering, Michigan State University

- 4 years' corporate procurement experience as follows:

1 year	-	Manager, Engineering Procurement
1 year	-	Senior Buyer, Engineering
1 year	-	Buyer, Specialty Chemicals
1 year	-	Associate Buyer, Packaging Supplies

As you can see, I have a broad smattering of procurement experience across a wide range of products (most of a fairly technical nature). My experience includes responsibility for the negotiation and management of multimillion dollar national contracts supplying some 50 Warner-Lambert manufacturing sites. Major contracts that I have handled include those at the $100+ million level.

During my four years with Warner-Lambert, I have been credited with savings in the $10 to $15 million range. This has resulted from a combination of skillful negotiations and exhaustive research to identify new, more competitive supply sources. Perhaps I could bring similar results to your company.

Should you wish to further explore my capabilities through a personal meeting, please call me at (313) 996-3189. I can be reached between the hours of 8:00 a.m. and 5:30 p.m.

Thank you for your consideration.

Sincerely,

Quentin D. Broome

Quentin D. Broome

KAREN B. LIVINGSTON

1901 Meadow Brook Road,
Midland, MI 28211

Email: KBLiv@AOL.com

Office: (715) 473-9872
Home: (717) 365-9876

May 30, 2004

Mr. William J. Meyers
President
Wilson Chemical Company
3500 West Parkway
Moorestown, NJ 19073

Dear Mr. Meyers:

I recently read an article in the *Chicago Tribune* about the enormous success of Wilson Chemical Company in the field of specialty chemicals and the major expansion you are planning. I would very much like to be a part of your future plans and feel I have much to offer a company such as yours as a senior procurement officer.

My qualifications:

- B.S., Chemistry, Ohio State University

- MBA, Finance, Northwestern University

- 20 years' procurement experience in the chemical industry

    - 2 years   Vice President, Procurement, Barlow Chemical Company
    - 2 years   Director of Procurement, Barlow Chemical Company
    - 3 years   Manager, Raw Materials Purchasing, Dow Chemical
    - 2 years   Manager, Chemicals Purchasing, Dow Chemical
    - 10 years Various Purchasing Assignments, Dow Chemical

My 20 years of professional and managerial experience as a procurement professional in the chemical industry has prepared me well for a high-growth company such as yours. I am up-to-date on the latest procurement systems and processes and could provide excellent strategic leadership to your procurement function.

Perhaps we could meet and jointly explore the many ways I could save your company considerable time and money. If you agree, please call me at (715) 473-9872.

Thank you for your consideration, and I look forward to hearing from you.

Sincerely,

Karen B. Livingston

Karen B. Livingston

WARREN J. TUCKER
201 North High Street
Holyoke, MA 06811
(204) 966-1701

February 22, 2004

Mr. Mark S. Samuelson
Director of Technology
Polaroid Corporation
One Kendall Square
Cambridge, MA 02139

Dear Mr. Samuelson:

I am a Research Engineer with six years' experience in the development of photo-imaging products used in the microprocessing field. Currently a key contributor to the Fort James Graphics' research effort in the micrographics field, my key achievements include:

- Lead researcher in the development of FJG's revolutionary new TEP microfilm technology.

- Development of new, non-silver halide film technology for use in consumer photographic market.

- Development of novel, new updatable microfiche for use in microfilm files.

My technical qualifications include:

- Ph.D., Polymer Science, M.I.T., 1998
  M.S., Chemical Engineering, R.P.I., 1996
  B.S., Chemical Engineering, University of Massachusetts, 1994

- Six years' R&D product and process development in photo-imaging technology.

- Awarded eight U.S. patents on new photo-imaging products and technology, with an additional 15 patent disclosures.

I am seeking a position as Group Leader or Research Manger, responsible for directing a product development team in photo-imaging research. Compensation requirements are in the $95,000 to $100,000 range.

Should my credentials be of interest to Polaroid, I would appreciate hearing from you. I can be reached at my home number most week nights after 7:00 p.m. Thank you for your consideration, and I look forward to hearing from you.

Sincerely,

Warren J. Tucker

Warren J. Tucker

CONSTANCE A. SHILLING

2408 Orchard Park Drive   Home: (708) 431-2176
Schaumburg, IL 60173   Office: (708) 255-1355

July 22, 2003

Ms. Karla B. Williams
Senior Partner
Search, Inc.
36 South Wacker Avenue
Chicago, IL 60606

Dear Ms. Williams:

Perhaps one of your clients is in need of a senior account manager for their corporate accounting operations. If so, they may well have an interest in my qualifications:

Educational Qualifications:

- B.A.,   Accounting, University of Wisconsin, 1997
- M.B.A.,   Finance, Michigan State University, 1999
- C.P.A.,   State of Wisconsin, June 2001

Professional Experience:

- 2 years' public accounting experience - Price Waterhouse Coopers
- 5 years' experience - Kimberly-Clark Corporation as follows:

        1 year   -   Assistant Manager, Corporate Accounting
        2 years -   Manager, General Ledger Accounting
        1 year   -   Accounting Supervisor
        1 year   -   Senior Accountant

I am seeking a position as Manager or Director of Corporate Accounting for a major manufacturing company reporting directly to the Chief Financial Officer. My compensation requirements are in the $90,000 to $100,000 range, and I am willing to relocate for the right opportunity.

I have an excellent performance record and am considered to be a "high potential" employee by my current employer. Unfortunately, I do not see a realistic opportunity for advancement in the foreseeable future. Outstanding references are readily available upon request.

If I appear to be a match for any of your current search assignments, please contact me and I provide you with a complete summary of my qualifications at that time. Thank you for your consideration.

Sincerely,

Constance A. Shilling

Constance A. Shilling

GEORGE W. BRUNSON
432 North Beach Court
Myrtle Beach, SC 13728
(614) 539-2406

March 20, 2004

Mr. Donald R. Bridges
National Sales Manager - Floor Coverings
Mannington Corporation
One North Main Street
Glassboro, NJ 17603

Dear Mr. Bridges:

What would you give to be able to hire one of the top sales representatives of your largest competitor? This is your chance!

I am the leading Senior Accounts Representative for Armstrong World Industries' Eastern Region. Major accomplishments include:

- National Sales Award – 2003, 2002, 2001, and 1999
  (top 10% of sales representatives nationally)

- Sales Rep of the Year Award, 2002
  (First Runner-Up, 2003)

- Increased territory sales volume by 600% in five years

I have been very impressed with your new ceramic tile line as well as other new floor covering lines you have introduced during the last two years. I feel that I could have major impact on your sales volume if given the opportunity to manage your Eastern Region. With my proven sales ability and your quality products and competitive pricing, I feel certain that I could lead Mannington to the number one competitor in the East in less than two years' time!

I hope that you can see the potential for an excellent marriage here and will give me a call. I would welcome the opportunity to meet with you to discuss the potential for making a significant contribution to your business. Of course, this inquiry is made in the strictest confidence.

Thank you for your consideration, and I look forward to the possibility of meeting with you personally.

Sincerely,

George W. Brunson

George W. Brunson

MARIAN E. FRAMINGHAM
202 Meadow Glen Road, Wilburham, MA 16273   *Phone: (712) 554-9823*

May 2, 2003

Mr. Daniel A. Parkinson
Director of Marketing
Borden Foods, Inc.
300 Borden Square
Borden, NJ 25378

Dear Mr. Parkinson:

Could your company use a talented, young Brand Manager with an excellent track record of double-digit annual sales increases achieved through highly innovative marketing strategies in the food industry? If so, you may want to consider bringing me in for an exploratory interview.

Please consider the following credentials:

M.B.A., Marketing, University of Massachusetts, 1997

B.A., Business Administration, Boston University, 1995

5 years' marketing experience, Friendly's Ice Cream Division.

2 years	-	Senior Brand Manager
2 years	-	Brand Manager
1 year	-	Associate Brand Manager

Key accomplishments include:

Led national marketing roll-out of new ice cream sundae line, achieving 60% market share in less than two years.

Revitalized sagging frozen yogurt line with change in name and packaging, coupled with creative advertising theme (55% increase in sales volume in less than six months).

Increased market share of powdered drink mix product line by 33 points to become brand market leader in one year.

I am confident that I can make similar contributions to Borden Foods and would welcome the opportunity to meet with you to explore the potential for a profitable career relationship.

Should you have an interest in my credentials, I can be reached at (712) 554-9823 during week nights. Thank you for your consideration, and I look forward to hearing from you.

Sincerely,

Marian E. Framingham

Marian E. Framingham

ALLEN D. MARKS
21 Lilac Road
Marietta, GA 30244
(404) 671-2066

August 15, 2004

Mr. Scott M. Beatty, President
The Bradford Group
Brandywine Corporate Center
Building 5
Malvern, PA 19355

Dear Mr. Beatty:

As an employment agency specializing in the field of Public Affairs, you may wish to be aware of my candidacy. Perhaps one of your client companies is looking for a talented professional with expertise in government and legislative affairs.

I hold a B.S. degree in Political Science from American University and have over five years' experience in the field of governmental and legislative affairs with Southeast Bell.

In my current position as Manager of Legislative Affairs for the states of Georgia, Florida, Alabama and Tennessee, I am responsible for the management of a staff of three professionals and am accountable for all state legislative matters affecting the business of Southeast Bell.

Some key accomplishments include:

- Led lobby effort that defeated Bill 334226 requiring a 3% Florida state sales tax surcharge on all local toll phone calls (annual savings $26 million).

- Initiated sponsorship, and led successful lobby effort, to pass Bill 44.5578A (State of Georgia) allowing Southeast Bell to provide long distance services within the state (annual sales revenue potential of $18 to $20 million during next five years).

- Defeated Tennessee House Bill 1996-344A, requiring the replacement of telephone and utility poles every 15 years (annual savings = $9 million).

Should you feel that one of your current search assignments is a suitable match for my qualifications, I would appreciate hearing from you. I can be reached most evenings at my home between the hours of 7:30 and 9:30.

Thank you for your consideration.

Sincerely,

Allen D. Marks

Allen D. Marks

TERRANCE T. JOHNSON

120 San Gabriel Avenue
Sunnyvale, CA 94086

TerrJohn@MSN.com

Home: (408) 296-4779
Office: (408) 703-9837

August 13, 2002

Mr. James H. Hoffman
Vice President Manufacturing
Mattel, Inc.
333 Continental Boulevard
El Segundo, CA 90245

Dear Mr. Hoffman:

The Mattel Corporation has always enjoyed an excellent reputation as one of the area's outstanding employers, and I have long had an interest in working for your company. Perhaps my dream has the potential to become reality!

I understand Tom Hardy, Operations Manager at your Pleasantville Plant, has just announced his retirement and that you are about to begin a search for his replacement. Perhaps I could save you the time! Please consider my qualifications:

- M.B.A., Finance, University of California, Irvine, 1991
  B.S., Mechanical Engineering, R.P.I., 1989

- Currently Plant Manager for Milton Bradley's Los Angeles Plant, a 350-employee toy manufacturing facility.

- Previously four years as Operations Manager for same facility.

- Fully versed in modern manufacturing concepts and approaches including JIT, MRP, high performance work systems, total quality, etc.

Since assuming the position of Plant Manager at Milton Bradley one year ago, I have brought significant improvements as follows:

- Reduced operating costs by 23% ($4 million annual savings)

- Led quality initiative with resultant 68% reduction in consumer complaints

I am confident I could make similar contributions to Mattel and would welcome the opportunity to meet with you personally to explore this possibility.

Thank you, and I look forward to hearing from you shortly.

Sincerely,

Terrance T. Johnson

Terrance T. Johnson

ELIZABETH B. DORAN

45 Goodwin Drive
Cherry Hill, NJ 08003
Home: (609) 223-4506

April 10, 2004

Mr. Neil K. Reid
Senior Partner
Heidrick & Struggles, LLC
6000 Madison Avenue, Ste. 450
New York, NY 10011

Dear Mr. Reid:

Some recent changes here at Sterling Winthrop have prompted my decision to make a career change. I am therefore sending this brief synopsis of my qualifications to your attention in the event one of your clients may be in search of someone with my credentials.

Highlights of my qualifications are as follow:

- Ph.D., Industrial Psychology, University of Texas

- 18 years' human resources experience in the consumer products (The Gillette Company) and pharmaceutical (Sterling Winthrop) industries

As Director of Human Resources for Sterling Winthrop's corporate staff, I currently report to the Senior Vice President of Human Resources and provide a full range of human resource services to the corporate offices (1,800 employees) of this $7 billion pharmaceutical manufacturer. In this capacity, I direct a staff of 36 employees with functional responsibility for human resources planning, staffing, organization design and development, training, compensation and benefits, and equal opportunity.

I am seeking a senior level human resources management position, preferably at the vice president level, with broad executive leadership responsibility. Although clearly secondary to job challenge and interest, my compensation requirements (base salary plus bonus) are in the low $100K range.

If this synopsis is of interest, I would be pleased to provide you with a more specific accounting of my qualifications during a face-to-face meeting. Should you wish, I can be reached at my office (Phone: 215-699-0717). Thank you.

Sincerely,

Elizabeth B. Doran

Elizabeth B. Doran

133 Puritan Road
Vienna, VA 12839

February 10, 2003

Mr. Mitchell D. Longstretch
Vice President of Human Resources
Subaru Corporation of America
19001 S. Western Avenue
Torrance, CA 90509

Dear Mr. Longstretch:

I am an experienced employment professional with solid training and experience in staffing for a Fortune 200 automotive company. Please take a brief moment to consider my qualifications:

- MBA, Human Resources Management, Michigan State University

- BA, Business Administration, University of Wisconsin

- Five years' corporate employment experience with The Alpha Automotive Corporation as follows:

  - 2 years = Manager of Technical Employment
  - 2 years = Assistant Manager, Administrative Employment
  - 1 year = College Relations Specialist

My staffing experience is broad, covering a wide range of business functions including marketing and sales, manufacturing, engineering, research, accounting and finance, human resources, public affairs, management information services, law and logistics. Additionally, I have handled all levels of recruitment from entry-level professional through vice president.

I am seeking a senior level staffing management position at the corporate level. Ideally, this would be either Director or Manager of Corporate Staffing. Should you have an appropriate opening on your corporate staff, I would appreciate the opportunity to meet with you. My office phone number is (310) 329-0900. Should you wish to reach me in the evening, my home phone is (310) 451-2910.

I look forward to the possibility of talking with you. Thank you for your consideration.

Sincerely,

Laura M. Drake

Laura M. Drake

7

Thank-You Letters

The previous chapters have covered the five types of cover letters frequently needed by job seekers. Certainly, however, there is one additional letter that deserves to be in any book dealing with the subject of cover letters or employment letters in general. This is the *thank-you letter*. It is the letter you should never forget to send if you want to ensure your employment candidacy is viewed in the most favorable possible light.

Far too often, job seekers overlook this basic courtesy in the swirl of activity that accompanies the job-hunting process. Yet, the favorable impression that is created by a well-written thank-you letter can speak volumes about the manners and character of the employment candidate.

While Manager of Technical Employment at a Fortune 100 company and later, while Vice President of an international executive search firm, I was surprised at the large number of employment candidates who, after a full day of interviewing, never dropped a line to either the employer or the search firm to say "thank you." This is a discouraging statistic, not to mention a real lost opportunity for the job seeker!

When you consider the time, effort, and expense organizations commit when hosting an employment candidate on interview day, it is certainly deserving of a basic "thank you." So, don't overlook this courtesy if you are interested in making a favorable impression and enhancing interest in your employment candidacy.

It is important to realize that besides displaying your good manners, the "thank you" letter offers a great opportunity to further market yourself for the position. Although this should not be the principal reason for writing the letter, it is certainly an added benefit worth taking full advantage of.

A well-constructed thank-you letter can go a long way to communicate not only your level of interest in the position, but also to reinforce your strong qualifications for the job. Additionally, it presents an excellent opportunity to highlight the special value the hiring organization will realize from bringing you on board. I have seen more than one occasion where well-written thank-you letters were the single deciding factor when the contest was down to the last two desirable finalist candidates.

ELEMENTS OF AN EFFECTIVE THANK-YOU LETTER

Review of the sample thank-you letters contained in this chapter will reveal a clear pattern. There are certain elements required to make such letters effective. These are:

1. Basic greeting or salutation.
2. Expression of appreciation for interview.
3. Statement of interest in position.
4. Value statement.
5. Restatement of appreciation for interview.
6. Close.

Normally, these elements are incorporated into the letter's construction in the order in which they appear here. The following thank-you letters, however, will illustrate some variations in how these elements may be used to your advantage.

120 Ridge Road
Raleigh, NC 18273

September 23, 2004

Ms. Martha T. Randolph
Director of Human Resources
Astar Corporation
1200 Commerce Drive
Atlanta, GA 16385

Dear Martha:

I wanted to let you know how much I enjoyed my recent trip to Astar Corporation and the opportunity to interview for the position of Engineering Manager. The day was certainly an informative one, and I appreciated the chance to meet with you and the other members of the interview team who all did such an excellent job of helping me to understand both the requirements of the position and Astar's work environment.

The position as Engineering Manager of your Pneumatic Products Division sounds like a challenging opportunity, and I wanted to reiterate my strong interest in this position.

In my discussions with Tony, he mentioned the primary thrust of this position; over the next two to three years will be the technology transfer of six new products which are critical components of the Company's business strategy. Technology transfer is, of course, an area where I have considerable experience, and I know I could be of real help to Astar in successfully bringing these products to market quickly.

Additionally, I feel I could provide meaningful assistance with your efforts to implement a corporatewide TQM program, since I was a key member of the corporate steering committee instrumental in implementing a highly successful TQM program here at Winston Company.

Again, Martha, I appreciated the opportunity to visit Astar Corporation. Please pass along my sincere "thanks" to the other members of the interview team who helped make the day such an enjoyable and informative one.

I look forward to hearing from you shortly.

Sincerely,

Thomas R. Reardon

Thomas R. Reardon

16 Delaware Overview
New Hope, PA 19283

June 16, 2002

Mr. Walter F. Baxter
Senior Vice President
The Richfield Company
Executive Search Consultants
4520 Park Avenue, Suite 1400
New York, NY 18773-1982

Dear Walter:

I wish to thank you for your time and hospitality during my visit to New York City this past Thursday. I appreciated your thoroughness in helping me understand the needs of your client for the position of Director of Marketing.

Although at this stage of the process I know it is customary for search consultants to maintain the confidentiality of their client, I did want to let you know of my preliminary interest in the position we discussed. It would appear to be an excellent match for my background and qualifications and certainly is "on target" with respect to my current career objectives.

My strengths in competitive intelligence should be of real interest to your client in their desire to launch a competitive intelligence function as a key component of their corporate marketing strategy. Additionally, my track record in the successful launch of several major consumer products (most of which have achieved either #1 or #2 in market share), should prove appealing to your client as well.

Based upon our discussion, I would welcome the opportunity to proceed to the next step. I hope you agree, and I will be hearing from you momentarily.

Again, Walter, thank you for your hospitality.

Sincerely,

Barbara A. Swanson

Barbara A. Swanson

D-14 Taylor Hall
North Carolina State University
Charlotte, NC 18279

February 22, 2003

Ms. Barbara L. Bradley
College Recruiting & Relations Manager
The Baxter Company, Inc.
22 Commerce Drive
Nashville, TN 83746

Dear Ms. Bradley:

I returned to North Carolina State after yesterday's interviews at The Baxter Company, thinking how exciting it will be to finally launch my career in Engineering and put my last four years of academic training to practical use. My visit with you and the other members of the interview team did much to heighten my level of interest and anticipation. What an exciting opportunity!

I wanted to let you know how much I appreciated the chance to interview with Baxter. I appreciated the efforts of both you and the other team members in making my day a very enjoyable and informative one. The position of Project Engineer, as described during my visit, sounds just like the kind of challenge that I am seeking at this early stage of my career.

Ms. Bradley, my strong academic achievement and interest in fluid mechanics would appear to be an excellent match for your needs. Although my interests are diverse, fluid mechanics has always been a subject of particular interest to me. My propensity for creativity, as supported by my background as an amateur artist, should also prove helpful. I look forward to working with Dr. Johnson on development of the new air-lay process, and the challenge of developing an entirely new, revolutionary way of manufacturing paper webs.

Please pass along my "thanks" to the other members of the interview team for their time and effort in providing me with a stimulating and interesting visit. I appreciated their thoroughness and patience in answering my many questions.

I look forward to hearing from you in the near future and hope your decision on my employment candidacy will be a positive one.

Thanks again for your hospitality.

Sincerely,

Loren L. Kingston

Loren L. Kingston

1512 Birmingham Road
Unionville, PA 12287

April 21, 2004

Mr. Irvin D. Bronstein
Manager of Corporate Accounting
Sampsonite Company, Inc.
1525 Executive Row
Claymore Business Park
Wilmington, DE 65291

Dear Irvin:

Thanks for the opportunity to visit with you this past Wednesday to discuss the position of Senior Tax Accountant on the Corporate Accounting Staff. I certainly appreciated your hospitality.

Since it captures so much of my technical strengths and professional interests, the position of Senior Tax Accountant, as described during my visit, is of great interest to me, and I would welcome the chance to further explore this opportunity with you.

Reflecting on our conversation, it would appear that I have most of the key qualifications you seek. In particular, my intimate knowledge of the tax aspects of the Alpha General Ledger System should prove additive to your efforts to painlessly launch this new general ledger system in October of next year. My background in international tax, especially in Europe, should also prove quite beneficial to Sampsonite's plans to start new ventures in both Germany and the U.K. I can certainly help you avoid some of the major and costly pitfalls from the tax standpoint.

All in all, I feel I have the necessary background and skills to be quite successful in the position of Senior Tax Accountant and would hope that you view my candidacy favorably. I am certain that I can make a real contribution to your organization.

Thanks again, Irvin, and I look forward to hearing from you shortly.

Sincerely,

Alan S. Stevenson

Alan S. Stevenson

D-216 Center Hal
University of Pennsylvania
37th & Locust Streets
Philadelphia, PA 19283

June 16, 2002

Mr. Michael Janson
Director of Marketing
Horwarth Beverage Company, Inc.
20 Industrial Court
Waymar Industrial Park
Denver, CO 16284

Dear Mike:

Thank you for the opportunity to visit Horwarth Beverage and the chance to explore the position of Associate Brand Manager for your new soft drink beverage, Quench. I certainly appreciated the hospitality of both you and the members of your staff, and the thorough way in which my interview was handled. The day was quite informative and enjoyable!

By comparison with most of the opportunities for which I am currently interviewing, the position of Associate Brand Manager - Quench sounds intriguing, and my interest is quite high. In particular, the chance to develop the complete marketing strategy for a new product, for a fresh MBA graduate, is exciting and is exactly the kind of opportunity for which I am looking.

As you are aware, I will graduate near the top of my class at Wharton with heavy course emphasis in marketing. My interest in consumer products marketing is especially strong. My educational qualifications, coupled with my prior marketing experience with the Kraft Foods Company, hopefully make me a particularly attractive candidate to the Horwarth. I feel I have both the training and motivation required for success in the consumer marketing field and that I have the potential to make substantive contributions to my new employer.

Thanks again for your hospitality during my visit, and please pass along my special "thanks" to the balance of the interview team for their part in making my visit a very pleasant and informative one.

I look forward to hearing from you and the possibility of further exploring career opportunities with the Horwarth Beverage Company. Thank you.

Sincerely,

Wendy D. Randolph

Wendy D. Randolph

8

Cover Letter "Do's and Don'ts"

This final chapter provides a basic checklist for use in evaluating cover letters you have written, before they are finalized and mailed. It provides a basic list of "do's" and "don'ts" that can be used as a last minute check to ensure maximum cover-letter effectiveness and impact.

COVER LETTER "DO'S"

1. Keep all cover letters to a single page, no exceptions!
2. Be brief and concise.
3. Eliminate any unnecessary words that add nothing to clarity or meaning.
4. Proofread for poor grammar, spelling, and typos; they can be deadly!
5. Always address letters to a *specific individual*, never to a general function.
6. Unless responding to an ad where instructions specify differently, always send letters directly to functional managers rather than the human resources or employment department.
7. Even where ads specify you are to send your response to human resources, do the necessary research and send a second copy directly to the manager of your target function.
8. Keep job descriptions brief and pithy.
9. Focus your letter on *relevant* results and achievements, not just job responsibilities.
10. Highlight significant accomplishments with bullet points; make sure they are seen!
11. Include compensation requirements, but only if you are certain they won't screen you out from an otherwise attractive opportunity.
12. Include geographical preferences or restrictions, but not if they are likely to screen you out from an otherwise highly desirable opportunity.

13. Except when using the resume letter, be sure to include a well-written resume as an attachment to the cover letter.
14. Stick to standard business letter formats; avoid the creative or exotic.
15. Use only commonly recommended type styles.
16. Make effective use of "white space," making your letter easy to read.
17. Use standard business paper, 20- or 24-pound bond, either white or buff in color.

COVER LETTER "DON'TS"

1. Never use a cover letter that is more than a single page in length.
2. Don't be verbose and ramble on-and-on.
3. Don't use unnecessary words that add little or no meaning to the core message.
4. Avoid allowing poor grammar, bad spelling, or typos to eliminate your employment chances.
5. Never address correspondence to a general function; always use a specific person's name.
6. Never send your cover letter to human resources or the employment function (unless required by an employment ad).
7. When sending your response to an ad, don't send it only to the human resources department. Always send a second copy directly to the management of the hiring function.
8. Avoid lengthy job descriptions in the cover letter. These can be boring and waste important space that can otherwise be used to market your value and key accomplishments.
9. Don't focus your cover letter on job responsibilities; instead focus the reader's attention on your key achievements and accomplishments (that is, your value).
10. Don't hide key accomplishments down in the bowels of the letter's text. Instead, highlight them using bullets and appropriate spacing to make them stand out.
11. Avoid highlighting mundane achievements.
12. Don't overcrowd text, making your cover letter difficult to read.
13. Don't include compensation requirements if this may possibly screen you out from a highly desirable opportunity in which you have a strong interest. Keep your options open!
14. Avoid including restrictive language that suggests you are geographically inflexible, especially when applying for that once-in-a-lifetime opportunity you've always wanted. You can always say no later.

15. Unless using the resume letter, don't send just a cover letter. Always include a well-written resume as an attachment.

16. Don't use strange or uncommon letter formatting; use conventional business formatting only.

17. Avoid using fancy or decorative type styles. Stick to conventional business styles only.

18. Don't use unusually lightweight or heavyweight papers; stick to either 20- or 24-pound bond (no exotic colors).

Index